ZUNI

A VILLAGE OF SILVERSMITHS

BY JAMES OSTLER, MARIAN RODEE, AND MILFORD NAHOHAI
PHOTOGRAPHY BY MICHAEL MOUCHETTE AND DALE W. ANDERSON.

Book designed by Sheila Edwards and Hisako Moriyama, Publications Office, Public Affairs Office, University of New Mexico. Photographs by Michael Mouchette and Dale W. Anderson. Electronic prepress and color correction of photo C.D. images by Anna M. Chávez, Aztec Media Corporation.

Produced by Zuni A:Shiwi Publishing and the University of New Mexico.

Printed in Korea.

Library of Congress Catalog Number 95-70836
ISBN: 0-912535-11-3 Hard Cover
ISBN: 0-912535-08-3 Soft Cover

Cover Photograph: Top left to right — Inlay necklace by Veronica Poblano. Ed Beyuka holding silver backing for inlay bolo tie. Wolf kachina pin by Andrea Lonjose Shirley. Turquoise needlepoint necklace by Bryant Waatsa, Jr.
Bottom left to right — Bracelet by Duran Gasper. Turquoise channelwork belt buckle by Jack Bobelu. Hummingbird bolo by Dennis Edaakie.

ACKNOWLEDGMENTS

With a tradition of Zuni jewelry making extending back more than a thousand years, and with more than a thousand currently practicing silversmiths, the immediate problem in writing a book about the rich history and the very creative present of Zuni is what do you leave in and what do you leave out; more precisely, who do you leave in and who do you leave out.

Our first acknowledgment is clearly to Zuni artists, to those who assisted us with interviews and with examples of their work pictured in this book, and also to those artists who for reasons of individual privacy or for reasons of professional modesty elected not to be interviewed or to have their work pictured. They are all preeminent artistic contributors to what the world has come to identify as Zuni jewelry.

This book is a collaboration among Zuni artists, a museum curator, a Zuni artist and entrepreneur, a Zuni trader, and two photographers. It is also a collaboration between an anthropology museum, a Zuni museum, and a for-profit enterprise of the Zuni tribe. We hope that it is only a beginning for Zuni artists to discuss their ideas and their art.

We would like to thank the University of New Mexico and fellow staff members of Marian Rodee, especially photographer Michael Mouchette, whose adaptability to unusual lighting and field situations was remarkable. Also thanks to Sheila Edwards, Hisako Moriyama, and Valerie Roybal of the UNM Publications Office for their patience and design and coordination talents.

Aztec Media Corporation, Dale W. Anderson and Anna M. Chávez, have contributed to this book with photographs and by steering us through the complexities of electronic imaging prepress in publishing this work.

Over the past several years many museums made their collections available to us for study and photography. They include the National Museum of the American Indian, San Diego Museum of Man, the University of Pennsylvania Museum of Archaeology and Ethnology, the Brooklyn Museum, the Laboratory of Anthropology of the Museum of New Mexico, the Wheelwright Museum, the Peabody Museum of Harvard University, the Museum of Northern Arizona, the National Museum of Natural History, and the Heard Museum.

At Zuni we especially would like to thank Josephine Nahohai for her gracious hospitality, and for sharing her knowledge and opinions about Zuni jewelry with us. We would also like to thank Mary Ghahate and Charles Hustito for allowing us to look over their shoulders in order to understand meanings and contexts for Zuni jewelry.

To the two Tribal Councils who served during the period that this book was being prepared we would like to acknowledge the open climate for Zuni scholarship which exists in part because of their own sense of inquiry and interest in Zuni arts.

Of course, we have a debt to our editors, Nigel Holman of the A:shiwi A:wan Museum and Heritage Center, Mary J. Piper, Tom Hall, and Kirby Gchachu, Zuni educator and linguist.

We would like to thank all the Zuni artists who put up with the silly questions of the Melika from Albuquerque, who analyzed the questions of their A:shiwi interlocutor, and for the praise, criticism, and opinions about Zuni art which they have generously shared over the past twelve years. Marian Rodee believes that she has finally found people who agree with her taste in jewelry, that more is better than less and bigger is better than smaller.

Were it not for the generous support of the National Endowment of the Arts, Folk Arts Division, and First Nations Development Institute this book and the exhibit it supports would simply not have been possible. At a time when programs for government support of the arts and scholarship are under attack we want to acknowledge publicly our indebtedness for this material support; we recognize that from the perspective of a place like Zuni Pueblo, the book and exhibit will clearly give knowledge of Zuni jewelry both to Zunis and to outsiders and this in turn will broaden the market for Zuni artists.

Lastly, we would like to say of the writers and photographers and those interviewing and interviewed in this book, thanks for picking up the slack when we were tired, thanks for making the project fun, and thanks for this record which we are pleased to share with others.

Jim Ostler   Marian Rodee   Milford Nahohai

CONTENTS

PART I

A Conversation between
Seniors and Milford Nahohai

Figure 1. Lolita Edaakie, Pearl Halusewa, Nora Leekity, Margaret Edaakie, and Frances Wysalucey

THE CONVERSATION WAS CONDUCTED IN ZUNI AND TRANSLATED BY LORETTA WEAHKEE AND MARY GHAHATE.

MILFORD: Why do you wear jewelry?

SENIORS: Because we have them. I guess just to wear as decorations (Fig. 1).

MILFORD: The other jewelry you wear, is there a reason why you sometimes just wear a necklace, and with other times you should wear everything? Why is that?

SENIORS: We like to wear stuff like when we have our special occasions going on, like Mudhead Payday. We like to dress ourselves traditionally—manta pins, bracelets, rings.

MILFORD: If you dress up traditionally without any jewelry, what will happen?

SENIORS: Nothing really, it's just when big events happen we like to wear our jewelry.

MILFORD: Why do we have jewelry, we Zunis?

Figure 2. Wayhusiwa, Zuni Governor 1923

Figure 3. Zuni delegation to East Coast in 1882

SENIORS: We really don't know but we sometimes make them or buy them. It is for decoration and it's like in the White ways, like life insurance.

A long time ago they used to wear white mantalike material and the ladies didn't have jewelry to wear until they started learning how to make jewelry.

MILFORD: What kind of jewelry would you sell and what kind of jewelry would you keep for yourself? How would you tell the difference?

SENIORS: The jewelry that would belong to you would be the manta pins (BIG), we would wear those only on special occasions but any other jewelry that's for sale does not have to be that big—rings, pins, bolos, earrings. If we make it for ourselves we usually make it a size bigger.

MILFORD: What about house jewelry? Do you lend those out to anybody?

SENIORS: We do give them out but mainly to relatives, and they usually return it after everything's over. If you give it to someone you don't know it might not return. Relatives will not only return it, but they will also give you blessings and you will be blessed with the same things and even more will be blessed with long life and good crops and a good future.

MILFORD: What makes Zuni jewelry look like Zuni rather than like Navajo?

SENIORS: I guess the designs. Some of the elderly buy Navajo jewelry because it is cheaper. They can tell the difference because the Navajos don't really do the inlay like thunderbird and hummingbirds.

MILFORD: When you reach the point where it is time for you to go, what would you wear?

SENIORS: You would wear only the expensive things that belong to you. You might want to leave things for the house and they would be handed down from generation to generation. Others might want to take it with them.

Really, it's whatever you own that you should take, but if you have already given it to the kids, it's up to the kids whether you are going to take it or not.

MILFORD: Why do you wear jewelry?

RITA: The jewelry I wear was given to me. I want to show the kind of jewelry we Zunis do.

MILFORD: Why would you wear jewelry like that?

RITA: I guess to look pretty.

MILFORD: I heard before that if you wear something "expensive" you are going to be "expensive," too. Have you heard anything like that?

RITA: Yes, because we are blessed with things, turquoise is valuable, with that you would be blessed . . . like we have turquoise in our cornmeal and with that we ask for blessings.

MILFORD: How do you tell which jewelry is for sale and which is for your own?

RITA: All the stuff I have are my own.

MILFORD: What about jewelry made in gold?

RITA: I don't wear gold all the time, only for special occasions.

MILFORD: If you want to buy anything for yourself, what do you look for?

RITA: How it's made, what it's made of, but if I like it I will buy it. If I don't like it I won't buy it.

MILFORD: What kind do you like—needlepoint or cluster?

RITA: I like to wear simple things when I go to work, but for special occasions, then I would like big stuff—"squashes, manta pins, long dangle earrings" (Figs. 2–7).

Figure 4. Bonnie Quam

Figure 5. Josephine Nahohai

Figure 6. Simon Bica

Figure 7. Chauncey Simplicio,
Zuni Governor 1983–1986

PART II

THE INSIDE AND THE OUTSIDE

BY JIM OSTLER

THE PLACE THAT IS ZUNI

ZUNI IS A RESERVATION, APPROXIMATELY FORTY MILES ON A SIDE, WHICH LIES ON THE WESTERN BORDER OF NEW MEXICO (FIGS. 8–16). ALONG ITS NORTHERN SIDE ARE NAVAJO SHEEP CAMPS AND ANGLO RANCHERS IN A CHECKERBOARD AREA. ON ITS EASTERN BORDER ARE MORMON RANCHERS AND THE RAMAH NAVAJO RESERVATION. ON ITS WEST-ERN BORDER ARE RELOCATED NAVAJOS IN "NEWLANDS" DEVELOPMENTS (A RECENT EXPANSION OF THE NAVAJO TRIBE) AND A FEW LARGE ANGLO LANDHOLDINGS. AND ON ITS SOUTHERN BORDER (RECENTLY EXPANDED BY THE ZUNIS) ARE MORE ANGLO RANCHERS. GALLUP, WHICH STARTED AS A RAILROAD TOWN IN THE 1880S, IS THE NEAREST CENTER OF COMMERCE AND LIES THIRTY-FIVE MILES NORTH ALONG INTERSTATE 40 AND THE TRANSCONTINENTAL RAILROAD. IN THE LAST TWENTY YEARS, GALLUP HAS BEGUN TO CALL ITSELF "THE INDIAN CAPITAL" (FIG. 12). ALBUQUERQUE IS THE NEAREST CITY AND LIES 150 MILES TO THE EAST.

Figure 8. Dance plaza

Figure 9. Ladder to roofs above dance plaza

Figure 10. Ovens near Mission Church

Figure II. Zuni River

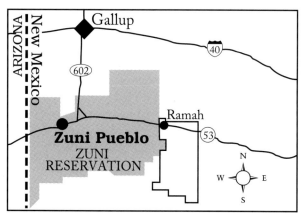

Figure 12. Map showing geographical relationships

Figure 13. Twin Buttes (*Kwili Yalanne*)

The Zuni River flows west from the Zuni Mountains—which lie along the southeastern reaches of the Rockies—through the farming village of Pescado and enters the villages of *Idiwan'a* and *Halona:wa* after about sixty miles (Fig. 11). In another thirty miles it flows into the Little Colorado River which then flows into the Colorado River before it drops into the Grand Canyon.

The reservation is a high plateau lying between six thousand and nine thousand feet. The higher areas of the reservation are covered with piñon, juniper, and ponderosa, the lower areas with sagebrush and grasses (Figs. 15–16). At lower levels, where water is available, corn, squash, and vegetables can be cultivated. In some areas fruit trees will prosper. The land is high desert with sporadic summer rainfall. Agriculture must be practiced in niches along the river, near springs, and where run-off from summer rains is sufficient (Figs. 17–20).

Most Zuni people continue to live in the valley of the Zuni River where Zunis have lived for the last thousand years. The language spoken in Zuni homes is *Shiwi' ma bena:we* which linguists describe as a linguistic isolate. The religion of the Zunis is the Kachina Cult which is enormously rich in its visual, theological, and auditory forms. It continues to hold the hearts and minds of the Zuni people, and continues to evolve. In civil matters, Zunis have their own constitutional government, courts, police force, school system, and economic base.

Figure 14. *Dowa Yalanne*

Figure 15. Ruins of the village of *Hawikku*

Figure 16. Landscape

Figure 17. Chile drying

Figure 18. Looking south over rooftops with corn drying

GOSSIP: THE TRANSMISSION OF STANDARDS

MOST INFORMATION AT ZUNI IS TRANSMITTED THROUGH A GOSSIP NETWORK THAT NOT ONLY GIVES DIFFERENT VERSIONS OF WHAT MAY HAVE TAKEN PLACE BUT ALSO PROVIDES THE "INSIDE"—THE CAUSE, THE MOTIVATION, THE REASON, AND THE FORECAST—FOR WHAT TOOK PLACE.

Figure 19. *Idiwan'a* with waffle gardens

The Tribal Government provides an organizational overlay for the village, primarily through its relationship to the federal government, its securing of grants, and the spending of those grants by its departments and programs. In many ways it operates more as an organizational chart on mylar film which maps activities of the village than it does to organize that activity. If the Council does not play a larger role, it is because real organization at Zuni comes through family, extended family, and clan. The Tribal Government's domain is the distribution of federal monies. Whatever directions or positions that it might take come largely from its constituents, who in turn cleave according to their family and clan.

Zuni is an oral society: beliefs, attitudes, criticism are largely expressed by actions and by spoken words—sometimes by silence—rarely in manifestos, treatises, or position papers. (A recent twist became evident on the eve of a primary election when a letter was mailed to numerous Zuni box holders denouncing one of the candidates. Upon receiving this letter some of the box holders then photocopied the letter and passed it among their gossip circle.) The entire community has a say on any issue, on any problem, on any criticism. Everyone listens to these opinions in their truest, and most democratically, revealed form—gossip. If there is a text for Zuni people, then it is gossip which provides the exegesis and the grounds for that text.

There is much of Zuni life that is theocratic, as evidenced by the sheer amount of energy committed to religious activities, to say nothing of time and money. When religious commitments call, it is the rare Zuni individual who does not listen. And if ill should befall the person who is neglectful, the cause of the ill is invariably explained in terms of what was not done, what duty had been neglected. Illness in the blemished life is thus easily understood.

Figure 20. *Idiwan'a* from the south

The ordinary stuff of Zuni gossip—the text—is material that is found in all gossip. Who did what to whom? When? And what did they then do? But the subtext of Zuni gossip is a debate on what it is to be Zuni. This is not an occasional pursuit, but one that is always at the forefront of Zuni discussion and criticism. Zunis have a clear understanding as to what is Zuni and what is not Zuni; a clear distinction as to how Zunis operate and how others may operate; a clear distinction as to what Zunis consider beautiful and what others may find beautiful. This analysis by Zunis is not made in terms of general theories and necessary deductions. It is expressed in individual statements and actions, denoting approval or disapproval, that are made about the actions of other Zunis. Thus, it is not a discussion carried on by intellectuals from whom

the rest of the village takes its cue; rather it is a continuing negotiation where all members of the community have an opportunity for their say.

This use of gossip as a means of conserving and creating culture (not just of admonishing miscreants) has most likely evolved because Zuni is an intimate community where inputs and results are immediate. Gossip has also been a means of holding the influence of outsiders at bay until they, their children, or even their grandchildren, have incorporated Zuni standards. Until that happens, the outsiders' views are dismissed as Anglo or Navajo or Acoma. For nonconformists and for slackers the most telling admonition is, "Tell them they are Zuni." What has been described is a culture being created out of the whole community, certainly not by an avant-garde portion, and this in turn helps to explain the conservativeness of Zuni society.

Though conformity to social norms by individual Zunis is certainly expected, Zuni society itself makes little effort to accede to the standards of others. For example, as one of its projects to stimulate the fetish market, Pueblo of Zuni Arts & Crafts, the tribal business, organized a traveling exhibit titled "The Fetish Carvers of Zuni." The exhibit traveled across the country for five years and was very well received. After it had been on the road for a year, a Santa Fe museum asked to be included. This museum has a review board composed mainly of Native Americans from Rio Grande Pueblos. One of their roles is to act as a conscience for the museum. After reviewing the exhibit, the board requested that a disclaimer be placed at the start of the exhibit stating that not all Pueblos approved of the public display of fetishes. Upon being informed that such a disclaimer would be unacceptable to Zuni, the board backed off their original demand and requested a letter for their files from the Zuni Tribal Council attesting to the council's support of the fetish exhibit. The head councilman at Zuni wrote to the museum stating that, as far as Zunis were concerned, what was being exhibited were carvings and not fetishes, that it was a display of Zuni artistry and that, although Zunis share many cultural traits with other Pueblos, Zunis have their own ways of determining what is appropriate and what is not. Nor does Zuni make much effort to change the minds of others. It does not proselytize, does not try to get others to see the "right" position, nor to follow the "right" religion nor to do the "right" art.

In a recent article in the *Wall Street Journal* titled "Rabbits' Feet Are Out of Luck: Carvings Are Charms of Choice," L.A. Winokur examined the current market in fetish carvings. She closed the article by writing:

> So what do the Zunis make of all this? Unlike some other tribal groups, "there hasn't been any real objection from the Zuni people to others buying these items and relying on them for direction," says Joseph Dishta, head councilman for the tribal council in Zuni.
>
> But, adds Mr. Nahohai of the Zuni arts and crafts enterprise, the Zuni prefer to think of them as carvings, "not fetishes in the true Zuni sense." To them, he explains, a carving becomes a fetish only after it has been blessed by the tribe's medicine society at the annual Winter Solstice gathering.
>
> "In our tradition, fetishes are used for things like healing, protection, spiritual guidance, good luck and longevity" says Lena Leki Boone. "A lot of my customers believe in that."
>
> "I believe in that," she says. "But, in my work I don't guarantee it."

Although others have described Pueblo societies as theocratic autocracies, Zuni does not easily fit this description. There are simply too many bosses. There are bosses who are charged with religious responsibilities in the six kivas, or in the seven medicine societies, or in the two fraternities. There are household bosses, women who own the houses and are charged with responsibility for the children. There are elderly matriarchs of the extended families who are sure of their models for raising good Zunis. There are religious advocates who impress with their oratory and are always in search of issues to catapult them to the forefront of Zuni life. There are elected political leaders who often serve only one four-year term. There are school administrators, tribal administrators, and department heads. There are artists and craftsmen known for their artistry and attention to detail. There are entrepreneurs. There are witches. Everyone in Zuni knows who they are and the import of their words on any given subject or any piece of gossip. There is an abundance of bosses at Zuni, some of whom are bosses all their lives and some who easily arrive at the position of boss and also easily leave it.

Any of these bosses may be—and in fact often are—autocratic in the niche in which they operate. In matters of religion, it is an expectation and a condition that they will be autocratic in the areas for which they are responsible. In civil matters it is expected that bosses will be autocratic, but it is not generally the wish of their constituents. This said, autocracy does not extend beyond its niche and rare is the attempt to extend it. For example, when a group of religious leaders (appointed by the tribal council to make recommendations regarding the protection of Zuni traditional cultural properties) were approached to give guidance on issues of tourism, they declined to enter the discussion saying that it was beyond the scope of their mandate.

On other occasions, when information has been sought about the appropriateness of using religious imagery, the answer invariably received was "I don't know—ask those guys" (who do have that responsibility).

Autocracy means a few bosses who are unelected. In Zuni, the bosses may be mostly unelected, but there are so many of them, and they have such specific roles, that their power—though strong in their niche—does not extend further.

Everyone at Zuni keeps their ear to the gossip network not only to find out what is being said about others, but also to discover what is being said about themselves. If an individual is unsure of how to proceed or how things are being perceived, the surest pulse of the community is the gossip network. It is a rare person who is not chastened by the network and does not amend his or her actions accordingly.

There is also a structural aspect to gossip. It must be lively, not prosaic, and must have the ring of credibility. It must hold interest and be about things and people that members of the network care about.

Gossip travels easily within networks but difficultly between them. The gossip network can be used by

any of the bosses to float trial balloons: by telling certain individuals, and knowing whom they will tell, it is possible to have ideas evaluated without ever publicly endorsing the idea or taking any public action.

These gossip negotiations work because of the compactness of the village (gossip spreads easily and the subjects are known to everyone), because everyone is Zuni (the cultural frames are well understood), and because of the preponderance of bosses (everyone has a say and wants to have a say). Furthermore, the system works for everyone, because everyone is part of at least one network. Gossip also has entertainment value—it is fun to send and to receive and it offers a break from the routine—like reading a newspaper about the people you know. But, the gossip is not really about truth, not really about facts, not even about people. Instead, it is about the values that Zunis hold important; and gossip uses the people who are known and their actions to illustrate these values.

Figure 21. Corn on a blanket

Just as Zuni corn appears to be a uniquely cultivated strain (Fig. 21), and the Zuni language is a unique strain, so is the Zuni value system similarly distinct from all surrounding groups. This singular value system underlies behavior and judgments, and there are clear and well-developed means by which these values are inculcated and reinforced. We will now examine how these values underlie and clarify Zuni art.

Figure 22. Drilling turquoise

Figure 23. Silversmith at a forge

IT IS EASIEST TO DESTROY A SOCIETY OR TO ALLOW ITS DESTRUCTION IF THE SOCIETY IS PERCEIVED AS HAVING LITTLE OR NO VALUE. IF IT HAS NO VALUE THEN THERE IS NOTHING TO SAVE; IF IT HAS LITTLE VALUE THEN THERE ARE FEW THINGS TO PRESERVE. IF THERE IS NOTHING TO SAVE, A SOCIETY'S PASSING REPRESENTS NO LOSS. IF THERE IS LITTLE TO PRESERVE THEN IT IS ONLY THE COLLECTING OF REPRESENTATIVE ARTIFACTS THAT NEEDS BE ADDRESSED. IN ONE CASE, IT MAY LEAD TO THE EXTERMINATION OF A SOCIETY, SUCH AS THAT OF THE NATIVE AMERICANS DURING THE CALIFORNIA GOLD RUSH. IN THE OTHER CASE, IT MAY LEAD TO THE ARCHIVING OF DISCONNECTED ARTIFACTS BY COLLECTORS AND INSTITUTIONS.

In either case, land, people, and their creations are usurped. In no small measure this has been the course Euro-American society followed in its encounter with the North American continent and indigenous people. There is still another way in which indigenous cultures can be usurped and that is the usurpation of native value systems. This is not a physical takeover, rather it is an intellectual one and occurs simply by subsuming the products of those indigenous value systems—art, religion, literature—under the dominant society's value system. In the Euro-American case, Native American cultural expressions were to be understood only in terms of Euro-American values and only those things that could be apprehended through Euro-American values were rewarded and encouraged, written about, and displayed. If it did not fit, it was ignored.

At the same time that America was destroying the Native American populations, some Americans were attempting to preserve the material culture of those societies. Pottery, clothing, and implements of war and religion were collected essentially as exotics, as quirks, as things that didn't fit but nonetheless held a certain "naive" charm. There were still other Americans that collected them as artifacts, as markers, sometimes as indexes of another culture that was seen as existing in a lower evolutionary state. In any case, for a material aspect of an indigenous society to be preserved it was either as an exotic or as an artifact of a "primitive" society or because it struck chords resonant with American values. There were no other reasons to give it attention.

This intellectual usurpation of Native American arts is still largely where we find ourselves in 1995. It is more than seventy years since the last Indian "war." No longer are Indian lands being taken outright, but we continue to see the arts of Native Americans either as curios or as art, more often as crafts, subsumed under the American value system.

Figure 24. Rolanda Haloo in her studio holding silver plate with cutout Rainbow Man to receive stone inlay

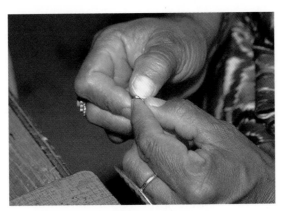

Figure 25. Bonnie Quam setting a bezel

Figure 26. Don Dewa

Figure 27. Rolanda Haloo holding a piece of coral

Figure 30. Myron Edaakie's studio

Figure 28. The Edaakie work table

Figure 29. Duran Gasper's closet workspace

Books on Native American art are written as if they were books on American art history, sometimes not recognizing—and not appreciating—that Indian arts come out of a separate history and out of separate cultural systems. Sometimes the position is taken that all art can be evaluated in the same ways, that ethnic origins have no bearing on our appreciation. Sometimes the position is taken that it is not art, but artifact, and only to be seen as representing a cultural phase. Sometimes the position is taken that its ethnic meanings will always be opaque, and what matters is how these ethnic objects have been incorporated into an American art system—as a Duchampian found object, for example.

Sometimes this type of book is appropriate because the meaning and content of the work, made by a contemporary bilingual and bicultural Native American, is intended for an American audience and accedes to their values—as in "authentic" Indian handmade, manufactured jewelry—or it was done in order to speak within an American value system to an American audience. In either case, the indigenous values do not have to be grasped because the work is produced for an American audience and therefore is stated in terms that audience would appreciate and understand.

It is difficult enough to understand art originating from one's own culture, let alone to understand it if it belongs to another.

Understanding art not only presumes knowledge of the genre—the family to which it belongs—it also presumes a willingness to unravel what is unique in the particular piece—the idiosyncracies of this particular

Figure 31. Josephine Nahohai polishing pottery in her living room

Figure 32. Kitchen work table

family member. Native American art-as-curio misses the family and the family member; as artifact it searches somewhat for the family and ignores the particular family member. Even though the apprehension of Native American art-as-curio or artifact may well block our understanding of indigenous values or the artist's contribution, at the very least it allows us a little appreciation and keeps us from being entirely indifferent.

What is unique about Zuni art is that it is not produced for an outside audience even though, in fact, most Zuni work is sold to a non-Zuni audience. Most Zuni art is exported from the pueblo to Gallup, Albuquerque, Santa Fe, Los Angeles, Phoenix, New York, Tokyo, Paris, and Frankfurt.

How can this be? If most Zuni work is sold to an outside audience, how can it not be made for that audience? Why is Zuni art an expression of Zuni values and not outside values?

There are plenty of immediate answers that can be given. Zunis by and large live in Zuni, and most Zuni work is therefore produced in Zuni. The village gossip network is very strong. The Zuni sense of values and aesthetics is very clear, with sharp boundaries. Most work is produced at home (Figs. 22–33). Most work that is sold is seen in the village. Most every family is a family of craftsmen and is both a promoter and a critic of Zuni work. All of these things are part of the system that the Zuni people have created to perpetuate Zuni work.

Figure 33. Alonzo Hustito with his daughter Erma in his studio

Jewelry As a Metaphor for Zuni Society

Figure 34. Coral bracelet by Lloyd Tsalabutie

Make yourself of value by wearing something of value.

—Josephine Nahohai to her son, Milford

This appears to be a moral statement about what her son ought to do and about how an individual may gain value by wearing something of value (Fig. 34). The implication is that value which is in Zuni jewelry will be transferred to the wearer.

This is not the way we ordinarily think about jewelry. In the world outside of Zuni there is costume jewelry, keepsake jewelry, and investment jewelry. The first has to do with presentation, the second with sentiment, and the third with monetary value. Josephine doesn't talk about what is valuable to an individual—as in sentimental value—but rather of value itself. We do not ordinarily think of jewelry's monetary value as transferring to the wearer. The Hope Diamond is valuable because of its rarity and the dollar amount that has been established for it. Though Elizabeth Taylor may wear it, the diamond makes her neither rare nor worth any given dollar amount. Thus, although owning jewelry may make one worth a certain amount, it is the owning that does it, not the wearing.

In Josephine's statement, on the other hand, it is the wearing not the owning that gives value. If selecting and displaying can be substitute words for wearing, then value in this sense may be closer in meaning to aesthetic value as understood by Americans. Wearing jewelry with aesthetic value implies that the wearer has an understanding of what is valuable and made the selection accordingly—that is, they have good taste.

Though this seems closer to what Josephine is telling her son, she is not just saying that her son should show that he has good taste. Rather, she

wants him to be valuable. Ordinarily, when we think of a person being valuable—of having value—the evaluation is based on what they do for others. Thus, a father has value for what he does for his son, a senator for what he or she does for their constituency, a Zuni for what he or she does for Zuni. If we are on the right track, then Josephine's statement is admonishing her son, saying, in effect, "You are a Zuni, make yourself valuable by showing that you are Zuni; show that you are Zuni by wearing what Zuni wears." Clearly, what Zunis wear, and what they ought to wear, is Zuni jewelry.

And why should Zuni jewelry be worn? It should be worn because it tells other Zunis and outsiders that the wearer is Zuni. It denotes what it is to be Zuni, and what is important for Zunis. It publicly displays to one and all what it is to be Zuni. It may even be a metaphor for Zuni society.

For other Indian tribes, Zuni jewelry may have taken an even larger role of signifying what it is to be Indian. At a recent conference in Maine promoting Maine basketry, nearly all the Native American basket makers in attendance—Maliseet, Pasmaquody, Micmac and Penobscot—were wearing Zuni jewelry. Men wore bolos and women wore needlepoint or inlay necklaces or pendants, in part, I think, to celebrate Indianness.

FIT

ONE OF THE FIRST THINGS TO NOTE ABOUT ZUNI JEWELRY IS FIT. TIGHTNESS OF FIT. EXQUISITE FIT. FIT BEYOND OUR EXPECTATION AND ALMOST BEYOND OUR UNDERSTANDING. FIT BEYOND WHAT WE WOULD EXPECT OF HUMANS WORKING WITH THEIR HANDS. FIT THAT IS ALMOST SUPERHUMAN. EVEN NEW WORDS HAVE BEEN INVENTED FOR IT—MICRO INLAY IS INLAY WHERE THE TOLERANCES BETWEEN CUT STONES ARE SO SMALL THAT THE NEW VIEWER OF ZUNI WORK CAN OFTEN MISTAKE THEM AS ENAMEL PAINTINGS (CHAMPLEVÉ) AND NOT AS AN INTRICATE MOSAIC OF STONES, EACH OF WHICH HAS BEEN CUT SO SHARPLY THAT THE BOUNDARIES BETWEEN THE STONES CANNOT BE SEEN (FIG. 35).

Figure 36. Wolf Kachina pin by Andrea Lonjose Shirley

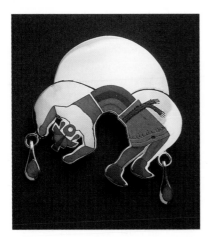

Figure 35. Rainbow Man pin by Rolanda Haloo

And how do Zunis describe this fit? They say the work is very clean, that the cuts are sharp and crisp, that the solder is minimal and not messy. And Zunis are very free with their praise for this kind of work, taking time to study the good examples and taking time to make public their admiration of such work.

Why this defining characteristic of pieces that fit? One could guess that the subtext for this Zuni jewelry is that Zuni is a society predicated on the fact that the pieces fit. Its individual members fit together to make a greater whole. Each piece that fits holds the other pieces together. The closer the fit, the tighter the whole. When any "stone" pops all the "stones" are in jeopardy of losing their fit and the whole piece may be lost. What one sees in Zuni jewelry are tiny pieces of stone, often of different colors, held together with very little metal. It is not so farfetched to see this as a metaphor for Zuni society where the members are held tightly together with minimal restraint and where each member depends on every other member to hold his or her position to make the whole work (see Figs. 35 and 36).

Niches and Specialization

IN NEEDLEPOINT EACH STONE HAS ITS OWN NICHE. IT IS THE AGGREGATION OF THE STONES, EACH IN ITS OWN NICHE, THAT MAKES FOR THE ELABORATED PIECE IN A NECKLACE OR BRACELET. EACH THIN AND POINTED STONE HAS BEEN CUT, SHAPED, AND SELECTED FOR UNIFORMITY OF COLOR AND SHAPE, AND EACH IS THEN SET INTO A TINY BEZEL WHICH HAS BEEN PREVIOUSLY SOLDERED TO A SILVER BACKING. EACH STONE IS THUS SET IN A ROW, IN A DISTINCTIVE, BALANCED, AND REPEATING PATTERN. WHAT EMERGES IS A PIECE OF JEWELRY THAT EXHIBITS CLARITY, PRECISION, CLEAN-NESS, AND ORDER (FIG. 37). CERTAINLY THIS IS TO BE CONTRASTED WITH UNCLEAR, IMPRECISE, DIRTY, RANDOM, AND DISORDERED. WHAT ALSO EMERGES FROM THIS INORDINATE PRECISION IS AN ALMOST MACHINELIKE QUALITY IN THE EXACTNESS OF DETAIL. ONE WONDERS HOW THIS JEWELRY CAN BE HANDMADE. NOT ONLY DOES EACH ELE-MENT OF A PIECE OCCUPY A DISTINCT NICHE, BUT THE CONSTRUCTION OF THE PIECE ITSELF EXHIBITS A CLEAR SPECIALIZATION THAT THE ARTIST/CRAFTSMAN HAS INVENTED. RAISED NEEDLEPOINT, FOR EXAMPLE, IS AN ELAB-ORATION ON AN ALREADY ESTABLISHED MEDIUM; IN THIS SENSE IT BECOMES A NICHE THAT THE ARTIST HAS CON-STRUCTED FOR HIMSELF (FIGS. 129 AND 130).

Zuni society can be described as a society of niches where members occupy clear and distinct positions of which they are master "boss" and maintain primary knowledge, responsibility, and control. Furthermore, each niche has its own specialist. Clearly, this is a way for a society to give worth to its members and, rather than evolving as a vertical society, Zuni has instead evolved as a horizontal society where each of its members occupies a necessary position or role and where each member must cooperate with other members to accomplish common goals.

It might be suggested that Zuni is a culture which rewards specialists: even the criticism heard at Zuni—the soldering is messy, the jewelry is not

clean, the dance group is unrehearsed—argues for the skilled practitioner and against the novice and the clumsy. Innovations occur slowly at Zuni, for they chart new aesthetic and technical territories and can be seen as clumsy. In Zuni silversmithing, for example, each new idea or technique is added incrementally to the family repertoire and each new piece is a finished, refined, and complete piece of art. Not only is there no place for messy work, the system for the creation of the work is such that messy work is precluded at the outset—consider-ably different from contemporary art schools where the student is encouraged to experiment.

Most silversmiths learn their craft as apprentices to their parents, an older brother or sister, or an uncle or aunt. In such a system there is clear reinforcement of the "right way" to go about the craft, and clear examples are given to the neophyte as to what constitutes good work. Typically, the beginning silversmith starts with easy tasks—like buffing or polishing—and learns the more difficult tasks after these are mastered. In this way, standards are maintained in the family's work—for a craftsperson only works according to his or her level of skill.

In general, a Zuni craftsperson gains reputation and respect through the specialties he or she has mastered—the silversmith known for his meticulously set, raised needlepoint; the potter known for his mastery of thin-walled vessels; the fetish carver known for his rendering of detail in stone; the miniaturist known for his finely rendered paintings measuring less than an inch across (Figs. 38a and b). Thus, it is within the specialist's niche that a Zuni may find his or her worth. In the case of a craftsman, it is the refinement of work that others can't do, and in the case of a religious leader it may be in having a responsibility for which he alone is accountable.

Typically, when an outsider asks about matters touching on religion—if it would be all right to do such and such—it is answered, "I don't know, ask those other guys." Such a response may be seen as simply a disinclination to take responsibility, but because it occurs so frequently it makes two deeper points. A Zuni does not claim to have knowledge outside his or her own expertise, and the specialization of those "other guys" gives them a sense of worth because of their irreplaceability. In the perfection of its handcrafted forms, Zuni arts also tend towards irreplaceability—there being simply no other craftspeople who can attain their level of lapidary skill.

There is also an ethic against copying other specialists. Within a family of fetish carvers, for example, a sister may say that her brother does mountain lions and that she could also do them but wouldn't without his permission. In the case of silversmiths, one will often hear a son or daughter say that they must

Figure 38a. Chris Natachu painting at his work table

ask their mother if they may use the designs of their deceased father.

The ways in which knowledge is transmitted at Zuni also leads to specialization. If a Zuni craftsman has no relative to watch and learn from he will probably not master the techniques and the grassroot technology to learn a particular handicraft. Thus one sees families that specialize in needlepoint, inlay, or cluster. To cross the boundaries—which is within the capability of any skilled craftsman—one nonetheless risks criticism for copying someone else's work or for sloppy, untutored work.

Figure 38b. Detail of Chris working on miniature

"Make yourself of value by wearing something of value." If Zuni jewelry makes the wearer of value because of what it means, it also may make them of value because of its material worth. There is clearly a sense of materiality in how Zunis wear jewelry, the preponderance of it, and the size of it. To an outsider this may suggest ostentation, abundance, even excess.

Figure 39. Preparation for *Shal'ak'o* house

THROUGH AMERICAN SOCIETY RUNS A PURITANICAL STREAK WHICH DOWNPLAYS INDIVIDUAL POSSESSIONS AND WEALTH. THUS, DISPLAYS OF JEWELRY ARE SEEN AS OSTENTATIOUS, AND AMERICAN MEN WEAR NECKTIES RATHER THAN BOLOS OR JEWELRY, AND BELTS MADE OF LEATHER RATHER THAN SILVER. IT IS THE NUANCES OF THEIR CLOTHING—THE CUT OR WEAVE—THAT SHOW EXPENSE, AND INSTEAD OF IMPUTING WEALTH WE COMPLIMENT THEIR TASTE. IN PART, THIS IS BECAUSE WEALTH FOR AMERICANS DENOTES PERSONAL WEALTH—AN INDIVIDUAL'S WEALTH RATHER THAN A FAMILY'S WEALTH OR A CLAN'S WEALTH—AND IT BECOMES SOMETHING TO BE CIRCUMSPECT ABOUT RATHER THAN CELEBRATE. IN ZUNI, HOWEVER, THE OPPORTUNITIES FOR DISPLAYING WEALTH BELONG MORE TO OCCASIONS FOR SHOWING THE GROUP'S WEALTH, AND THUS HAVE MORE TO DO WITH DISPLAYING GROUP SOLIDARITY AND STRENGTH THAN AN INDIVIDUAL'S POSSESSIONS (SEE HOUSE JEWELRY, FIGS. 40–43).

Figure 40. House jewelry

One of the remarkable events of the Zuni religious calendar is Mudhead Payday. On this day the central plaza becomes a holding ground for collecting, displaying, and rewarding material gifts to the ten Mudheads. Individual Mudheads stand impassively along the perimeter of the plaza, a Pendleton blanket wrapped around them. Behind them, clan members pile their gifts in huge stacks as high as the surrounding rooftops. Bags of flour, Pendleton blankets with money sewn into them, Navajo blankets, jewelry, television sets, VCRs, baskets of food, and utensils make up the piles.

These enormous piles of material are not tokens of obligation; they are outpourings of materiality by people who care, who participate together in the ceremony, who give and receive blessings, and who are paying back their Mudhead for his year of religious service. Materiality becomes the means by which individual Zunis tangibly show their gratitude, their affection, their respect and their solidarity with their Mudheads and their clans and also as an expression of and commitment to what is Zuni.

Sha'lak'o houses also display an abundance of goods—rugs, jewelry, blankets, mounted animals—which mark the area in which the *Sha'lak'o* move and participate in blessings for the earth's renewal and receive those blessings as well (Fig. 39). In a similar way, the members of the Zuni marching band—heralded as The Million Dollar Band—wear their families' squashes and concho belts in their performances and thus continue the premise of sharing wealth as a group.

Figure 41. House jewelry

Figure 42. House jewelry

Figure 43. House jewelry

Figure 44. Robert Leekya at work

The Economics of Specialists: The Making of Zuni Art

Crafts produced at Zuni reveal a community of more than one thousand artists/craftsmen/entrepreneurs who work in their homes making jewelry, fetishes, pottery, paintings, and beadwork. Hundreds of small workshops have been set up in outbuildings, garages, rooms off the kitchen or dining room, or even on a kitchen table that is cleared of tablecloth and dishes.

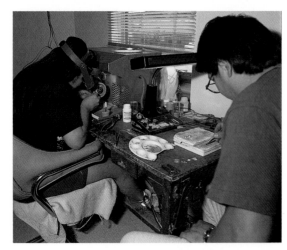

Figure 45. Ferdinand and Sylvia Hooee in their work space

No matter how small the space, it is organized efficiently with tools and equipment close at hand and supplies on shelves, in jars, boxes, and tins (Figs. 44 and 45). The workspace is geared for volume production; it is not one pendant that the silversmith works on but a dozen, not one pot awaiting polishing but a half dozen, not one stone the fetish carver is rough carving but a dozen. Typically a silversmith finishes all the silverwork for a number of pieces before setting any of the stones and will set all of the stones before polishing any single piece. Zuni craftsmen tend to work in multiples—in dozens and sometimes multiples of a dozen. If a buyer wishes to order four pendants, for example, he will usually have to wait until the craftsman has put the final touches to a dozen or more pieces. Arts and crafts at Zuni is a cottage industry and each household is geared for the production of certain kinds of work—needlepoint or inlay or cluster in jewelry, or pottery, or fetish carving. What this usually means is that a husband and wife and their children have organized their work to take advantage of labor-saving techniques.

Work as a group activity, production in numbers, and efficiency of volume production are common in Zuni work and are likely to have come out of social patterns developed in extended family and farming communities. These same patterns for example are also demonstrated by Zuni bread making. Although bread making has a social component (bringing the extended family together to prepare food for religious events) that making jewelry does not, still the economic patterns that come out of an activity like bread making—mass production, large quantities, graduation of tasks, apprenticeship—have a clear parallel in the making of jewelry.

Zuni bread is baked in quantities of twenty-five to 150 loaves with three to ten women doing the baking (Fig. 46–48). When bread is baked only for the immediate family, a mother and daughter will

Figure 46. Bread cooling in *Shal'ak'o* house

Figure 47. Bread cooling

generally use one oven and bake from twenty to twenty-five loaves in a single batch. When bread is baked for social or religious occasions, as many as ten women, usually relatives, will fire up to ten ovens and bake up to 150 loaves. Zuni ovens are built in clusters of five or six to facilitate this mass baking.

Mary Ghahate was asked if she ever baked bread in a kitchen oven. She said that occasionally she would, but that "it takes too long." A kitchen oven is capable of handling four loaves at a time while a battery of Zuni ovens can bake 150 loaves.

Another point to make about Zuni bread making—and Zuni crafts—is that efficiency of volume production may require three to ten workers of various skill levels. It is, however, through the interaction of older and younger craftspeople in the same project that technical knowledge is passed on. Thus, by assisting in bread making, the novice learns how to make starter, how to mix dough, how to shape it and let it rise, how to fire ovens, and how to clean and cool them to the right temperature with cedar boughs dipped in water.

Figure 48. Retrieving bread from oven

The novice learns to assess temperature by how quickly the *kyadochi:we* (bran or meal) browns on the hot oven floor, and how to load the ovens and then unload the hot bread.

Making Zuni arts essentially means working at home, in one's own space, according to one's own schedule, and with other family members where an established division of labor exists. Though there are manufacturers in Gallup and other neighboring towns that make Indian jewelry, there are few Zunis who work in this sort of manufacturing facility or who do piecework for them. Perhaps Zunis do not gravitate to the jewelry factories because working at home allows a freedom and creativity that the manufacturer's setting in a nearby town does not.

If an order is large or the market high, additional family members can be brought in to share the work according to their level of skill. The activities of the day follow a less regimented schedule than the typical workday. Children can be cared for, livestock tended, gardens cultivated, neighbors and relatives visited, and religious activities participated

in according to the Zuni calendar. It means that there is no boss other than oneself, and that one's income is a direct result of work completed and the skill and artfulness of that work. If burnout occurs, the craftsman can take a day or a week or a month or even a year off. Working at home also means that the Zuni artist/craftsman is the entrepreneur, the production manager, the craftsman, and the artist for his own work and sets his own price. The skills and techniques a craftsman develops for setting and polishing stones, and whatever new designs he originates, belong to him. They are his job security and to a degree his retirement fund.

How does it work? How does the outside meet the inside in today's Zuni? The first thing is that the outside has to come to Zuni (Fig. 49). Though there are a few Zunis who live outside the village and will sell their work, if the outsider wants to meet Zunis the burden is usually on him to come to Zuni. There are exceptions, such as the Gallup Ceremonial and the Santa Fe Indian Market; a few Zunis do live in Tucson, Seattle, and Albuquerque and will sell their own and other Zuni work.

Figure 49. Buyer's car behind firewood

Figure 50. View from the south of *Idiwan'a*

IN SOME WAYS ZUNI HAS CONSTRUCTED
ITSELF—AND HAS SURVIVED—AS A CULTURAL
ISOLATE. THIS IS NOT TO SAY THAT ZUNIS
ARE ISOLATED, NOR THAT THEY DO NOT TAKE
IN FROM THE OUTSIDE. RATHER, IT IS TO SUG-
GEST THAT IN PART THEY HAVE DISTIN-
GUISHED THEIR SEPARATENESS FROM ALL
OTHER PEOPLE AND SEEM TO ACT IN THE
BELIEF THAT THEIR ULTIMATE SURVIVAL
DEPENDS ON IT.

Figure 51. Rooftops with drying corn

The area where Zunis live is not particularly hospitable: rain falls infrequently and sporadically, soils are of marginal fertility, and the growing season is short. It is a place that can support a modest number of cattle and sheep, modest agriculture, and some timber cutting (Fig. 50). In the surrounding countryside, for a hundred miles in any direction, there are very small towns of a few hundred in population—Snowflake, St. Johns, Ramah, Thoreau, St. Rafael, Acoma— all widely separated. Between them is a land largely unpopulated. The exceptions are Gallup and Grants. Both straddle the railroad and Interstate 40 and have become cities and commercial distribution centers in this century. Excepting them, there is nothing in this region of sparse resources which focuses a population as does Zuni (Fig. 51).

It is called *Idiwan'a*—the Middle Place—a name implying significance quite beyond its material resources. Zuni has been created and maintained in no small part because the Zuni people see themselves as separate, as being a separate people, as living separately, and as surviving because of this separateness. They have a different religion, a different language, and different ethics and aesthetics from every other people. This begins to explain why one doesn't find a large expatriate population in Gallup, Albuquerque, or Phoenix. And it may begin to explain how it is that a population can be maintained in a land disproportionate to what that land normally carries in population density. Not only is this the only place one can live as a Zuni, it is the only way to be Zuni. To leave is to risk forfeiting what it is to be a Zuni. And for many, to leave is to risk forfeiting Zuni.

The tradition is that traders and travelers come to Zuni—and they still come—to buy, to witness ceremonies, to sell, and then they are gone. They come as Anglos, Navajos, Hispanics, other Pueblos; from Europe, India, and the Middle East. A few may stay, living as outsiders and performing some discrete function as an intermediary or administrator. A few are married to members of the tribe, their children

somewhat marginalized, and perhaps their grandchildren or great-grandchildren becoming more Zuni. Still the memory lingers that something other than Zuni is in their blood, that some values other than Zuni may be espoused by them. Navajos have created new clans because of mixed marriages—the Mexican clan, *Naakaii Diné,* the Zuni clan, *Naasht'ez'hi Diné*—and view mixed parentage as a source of pride and richness. One does not hear anyone from Zuni refer to their mixed ancestry. Instead, one hears that marriages between outsiders and Zunis may end the family line.

Zuni also demonstrates the strength of being a cultural isolate. The ground is very clearly marked. All within know the territory. They not only know how to behave, but know what to expect and what is good and what is beautiful. There is no confusion about values. There is no agony of reappraisal or of charting new directions. The model for new cultural and social expression becomes an elaboration of what went before—not synthesizing, nor interpreting, but elaborating the Zuni details that are already known. Thus, there is no room for the avant-garde in Zuni. There is nothing to rebel against, there is no randomness to interpret, there are no leaps into the unknown, for there is no value on the fringe, no value in the disconnected.

If there is crisis in Zuni life it is not about what direction to take, but rather about how to live up to expectations. Thus, the creativity that is Zuni is not that of overhauling a system and certainly not the positing of a new one. The creativity for any Zuni lies in the same place as the power—in the niches.

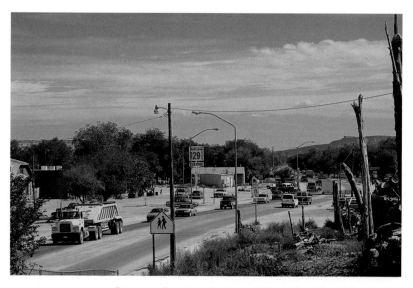

Figure 52. Downtown Zuni, view to the northeast from *Idiwan'a,* 1994

For the first-time visitor to Zuni it may take a while to see what is remarkable and it may appear that the village is a loose aggregate of houses which lies thirty-five miles south of Interstate 40, quite separate from any economic network. The visitor may be surprised at what appears to be a disproportionately large number of jewelry stores for a village this size, and it may not be readily apparent as to why this should be the case. Consequently, Zuni may appear at first glance to be a village without industry, without concern for acquiring it, and without a strong tradition of it (Fig. 52).

On the question of strong tradition: consider that the language of the Zuni people is spoken by less than eight thousand people and that no other People speaks a language even related to Zuni. The implication is that a group of Zuni speakers have lived very independently for a great time surrounded by non-Zuni speakers and cultures.

When two Zuni ladies were asked if they ever had a job where they could not speak Zuni, they quickly responded that, "It wasn't so bad because they could speak Zuni at home." What also came out in this discussion was that not only was Zuni the language of home, it was also the language of

social occasions and the more people to whom Zuni is spoken the larger the family. Thus, the Zuni language is a means of reinforcing kinship with other Zuni speakers.

On the issue of industry: consider that out of a total tribal population of 8,588 (July 1994) more than one thousand are craftspeople earning a majority of their income through the sale of their arts. (It is interesting to note that seven-eighths of the enrolled tribal members live at Zuni.) Lastly, consider that knowledge of Zuni arts extends far beyond the reservation, New Mexico, or even the United States. Zuni arts are sold in stores around the world. Consider that there is a café called Zuni in San Francisco and another in Australia, a grill in San Antonio, and tribally owned stores in San Francisco and Los Angeles. Finally, consider that an importer of textiles from India has taken to calling his line "Zuni." The implication is that the word "Zuni" is becoming a word which is used on non-Zuni goods to signify cultural uniqueness and excellence.

These bare facts tell a remarkable story of cultural conservativeness, independence, and a story of meticulous artistry and the willingness to trade objects that are the product of that artistry.

My sense is that these are not traits the Zunis learned when Coronado initiated sporadic Spanish contact in 1540, nor when the Americans established reservations in the Southwest after the Navajo Wars, nor when the railroad was built and a town grew up around a paymaster named David Gallup, nor even when a group of Gallup businessmen lobbied to have the interstate highway come through their town. These features of Zuni life are symptomatic of Zuni values and have considerable antiquity in Zuni history and prehistory—the Chaco road system extends as far south as Zuni. My sense is that the ways in which Zunis now deal with the outside world are in fact the ways that Zunis have long dealt with outsiders: with self-confidence, without fear of strangers, willing to trade, and sure in their values and their artistic expression of those values.

Zunis are not great travelers. There are no Vasco de Gamas or Marco Polos among them. Many have not gone beyond Holbrook to the west or Albuquerque to the east. Ask young Zunis if they have been to Flagstaff or to San Francisco and they might say, "Well, if I had a car I would go there." The answer is more fundamental—there is a rootedness to Zuni.

One gets the impression that Zunis are living in the right place, among the right people. What they require is close at hand, and if something is needed it will eventually come to them. Their vision of things does not have to do with Crusades to some distant land, nor with going to some distant place to seek a vision. Instead, it has to do with righting the world from *Idiwan'a*, the Middle Place. Furthermore, the place where Zunis go when they die—*Kǿuwala:w'a* or Zuni Heaven—lies not more than forty miles from the village. And one might not unfairly suggest that the Zuni vision comes out of practicing agriculture in a land of sporadic rainfall, and that it focuses on nurturing what is close at hand (Fig. 53). At Zuni, this takes the form of operating in a prescribed area, in a limited scope, and understanding as far as it is possible for anyone to understand how it is that things grow and die and how they can be assisted. This is an interest in using a limited area with the application of limited means. Certainly this stands in contrast to people who feel that the next real excitement lies beyond the next mountain range or the next ocean. For Zunis, the excitement is in *Idiwan'a* and has to do with what individuals do—the gossip network— and what religious societies do—the Zuni commitment to a sense of order beyond the individual.

Zunis tend not to look elsewhere for direction or inspiration. Criticism that is heeded tends to be criticism that comes from within the village. Criticism from without is more or less dismissed as not being relevant to life at Zuni or to Zuni values. At Zuni one often hears, "Others may do that, but this is not what we Zunis do."

Zuni is a remarkably autonomous society which has defined itself in its own terms for a long time and continues to do so. Although it has incorporated material goods from other places, it uses them as it has in the past—to make life easier or as raw material in the expression of their art and their traditional beliefs.

Figure 53. Waffle garden agriculture

Figure 54. Selecting coral

THEY COME IN THE FORM OF TRADERS, TEACHERS, ADMINISTRA-
TORS, HOSPITAL INTERNS, AND BUREAU OF INDIAN AFFAIRS OFFI-
CIALS. TRADERS, HOWEVER, ARE NOT SO MUCH TRADERS—THAT
IS, THEY HAVE NO GOODS TO EXCHANGE—AS THEY ARE BUYERS.
TEACHERS MAY BEGIN AS OCCASIONAL RETAIL BUYERS—COLLEC-
TORS—AND GRADUATE INTO WHOLESALE BUYERS WHO RESELL
THEIR PURCHASES. ADMINISTRATORS IN THE HOSPITAL OR IN THE
BUREAU OF INDIAN AFFAIRS TEND TO STAY WITHIN THEIR PRO-
FESSIONAL NICHE AND DO NOT GO BEYOND THE ROLE OF COLLEC-
TOR. WHEN THEY FINISH THEIR TOUR—AFTER TWO OR THREE
YEARS—THEY GENERALLY LEAVE THE PUEBLO.

Figure 55. Shell for inlay

Nowadays, goods are generally quite accessible to
the Zunis and therefore do not require a trader to
secure those special items which he will use to
exchange for goods that Zunis possess. Generally
trade has been supplanted by purchases on both
sides. In this new purchase-oriented context the
buyers have gotten larger and so have the suppli-
ers. Though there is money to be made in both
directions by trading, it is usually the small dealer
trying to squeeze more profit or the more rapa-
cious large dealer attempting to corner the market
in some new item who continue to trade. The
terminology has also changed—the word "trader"
being replaced by "buyer" or "dealer." "Buyer"
implies a smaller transaction, often of a more
personal nature. One hears craftsmen refer to an
individual as "my buyer." "Dealer" implies more
capital and perhaps a less personal relationship, in
that the dealer may be able to buy a family's total
production, or many families' production, and may
switch from family to family depending on the
market and price at which something is offered.
Thus, the dealer may offer a harder bargain than
the buyer, but may be able to buy much more. The
dealer is apt to try to negotiate a better price from

Figure 56. Water buffalo horn for fetish carvers

Figure 57. Polishing compounds

the craftsman—though in good times this is often ineffectual as there are so many competing buyers and dealers. The dealer is also more likely to treat the jewelry as commodities, looking for large numbers of pieces to be replicated, dealing with large numbers of craftsmen and probably being less loyal to any given craftsman. The buyer, on the other hand, is more likely to be searching out the singular, the highly crafted, the polished, the creative, and will offer premium prices for such pieces. Some buyers only look for exotics: the rare, the unusual, and the idiosyncratic.

The trader may also have searched for exotic raw material to trade, for which he will exact high prices from the craftsmen. Some dealers will also specialize in supplying materials such as lapis, coral, red shell, or turquoise (Figs. 54–58). Generally these dealers do not sell raw materials directly to craftsmen— the volume to individuals is too low—but will come to Zuni to make deals with the dealers who buy Zuni goods. Sometimes the deal is struck in trade but more often it is in cash. These dealers in raw materials may come to Zuni from China with turquoise, from Spain with coral,

from Mexico via Gallup with red shell, from Afghanistan or Germany with lapis, and will provide raw stones, cut stones, and beads.

Occasionally buyers or dealers will provide materials to craftsmen. The intention is to give the craftsmen access to good materials and to ensure that the finished products are offered back. Some dealers will work to corner the market in a particular raw material and supply only those craftsmen whom they believe can be trusted to not sell the finished items to competitors—in this way ensuring their corner on a segment of the arts and crafts market. Though this is often the preoccupation of some dealers, its success is generally short-lived as all the other dealers are keen observers of the market and quickly discover what is selling well and their own sources for the new material. Both craftsmen and dealers know that access to good quality materials is a most important ingredient for the marketing of any Zuni work: lapis that has good color and luster, coral that is deep red and not ridden with cavities, turquoise that has good color and will take polish. Consequently, most craftsmen and most buyers prefer natural materials. Doctored,

or artificial materials, though available in Zuni, are generally not used. The reputations of both dealer and craftsman are built on supplying works of fine craftsmanship which make use of good quality materials. Occasionally artificial materials are introduced in Zuni work; they are quickly detected by the artist/dealer network and the word is passed on as to what to look out for. Artists don't want other artists undercutting their price through the use of cheaper, artificial materials, and dealers don't want other dealers to undercut their prices. Outside this knowledgeable network the buyer must beware.

Dealers at Zuni in recent years have taken to posting signs at point of purchase that they will not buy jewelry containing synthetic materials. Though the State of New Mexico has developed fair trade laws to protect the consumer against fraudulent Indian jewelry, generally there has been little more than token enforcement. There are also federal laws on the book governing the fraudulent sale of Indian jewelry but, three years after the enactment of this legislation, the Indian Arts and Crafts Board has yet to come up with any regulations and so the law is unenforceable. At Zuni, where craftsmen and dealers are keenly aware of the market interest in genuine goods, buying and selling is largely self-regulated. This is so because buying at Zuni is not an occasional activity but in fact is marked by continuing transactions. An occasional tourist might be hoodwinked to nobody's detriment (except the tourist's) but for a craftsman to deceive his buyer or dealer, and for the dealer to deceive his buyers, is to jeopardize a critically important business relationship. This is not the case for the Indian jewelry industry at large where transactions are more occasional and occur in settings where buyers and sellers have less knowledge of each other. In Zuni, buyers and sellers may deal with each other for decades on a weekly or biweekly basis.

It is more by fortune than by design that tourists meet Zuni craftsmen. Though there are a few retail shows in which Zunis participate, even some in

Zuni itself, the volume of sales is marginal in comparison to the sales to buyers and dealers. The Zuni jewelry industry has developed as a cottage industry where Zuni families are the craftspeople and are capable of producing large amounts of work which can easily be sold within the village. When the worldwide appetite for authentic, Indian handmade jewelry is high, the cottages can generally sell their work to dealers and buyers within the village. In contrast to selling to tourists, profit margins are low but quantities large—but selling time is minimal, requiring only a short drive across the village. The retail buyer, the tourist, has to be given knowledge, made comfortable, has to be talked to, in short, has to be cultivated in order to make the sale. Also there may be a lot of waiting time between customers. Though profit margins may be high on each piece, gross sales may be low and there's a lot of time spent selling that can't be spent making. Many craftsmen at Zuni can sell all of their work to buyers and dealers even before it is made and, for these craftsmen, dealers will place orders and make advance payments. They can also send another member of the family to deliver their work, and young children can be seen delivering the goods and picking up cash or a check for transactions totalling several hundreds of dollars.

It is profitable to deal directly with tourists in venues like the Santa Fe Indian Market or the Museum of Northern Arizona, and some of the better known craftsmen set up booths for two- or three-day events. But generally the impact of tourists is small.

Unlike at other pueblos, there are no signs in Zuni windows indicating that silversmiths are at work and inviting tourists to come into the house. Instead, what one finds are a half dozen stores with large displays of merchandise, and assorted vans, cars, and motor homes parked below the old part of the village. Novice buyers will post hand-printed buying signs in their vehicle windows. More experienced buyers have certain areas staked out and conduct their buying with regular hours once or twice a week; they become known on the street and their sellers can easily find them. Other buyers follow regular weekly schedules, eat their lunch in the same place and at the same time, and will follow a routine by stopping at the homes of a particular group of craftspeople. The relationship is marked by reciprocity: the buyer comes to depend on the craftsman's work as part of the inventory for which he is known, and the craftsman comes to depend on his buyer's purchases.

Better-known craftsmen making high quality goods rarely sell them on the street. Generally it is the lower-end earrings, pendants, and bracelets, of good craftsmanship but of more repetitious designs, that are sold on the street. Thus, in this market one sees identical pendants, bracelets, or pairs of earrings being sold over a long period of time. The craftsmen's tactic is twofold: to space their visits to the buyer at appropriate intervals, and to solicit as many new buyers as possible.

Generally, it is the more itinerant buyers who accommodate the street trade. Dealers, on the other hand, particularly when they have stores in Zuni, are easy to find and have cultivated relationships with particular craftsmen and will buy their work whenever it is presented. Such relationships are marked by the frequency of the visits and the ease of the transactions. There is almost no negotiation as everyone knows the price, and there is almost no checking of quality as everyone is aware of the reputations involved.

Figure 59. Billboard in Gallup

CLEARLY WHAT IS MADE IS MARKET DRIVEN. IF A DESIGN WON'T SELL IT MAY BE WITHDRAWN BY THE CRAFTSMAN WHO WAITS FOR AUSPICIOUS TIMES. WHAT IS MADE IS MADE TO SELL, AND IF IT DOESN'T SELL IT IS NOT MADE. BUT, THIS DOES NOT MEAN THAT ANYTHING IS MADE. IT STILL HAS TO FIT THE PERVASIVE STANDARDS THAT ARE ZUNI.

Gallup is a commercial center which succeeds largely because of the Navajos and Zunis who come to town to buy a car, furniture, clothing, or food (Fig. 59). In the last ten years it has developed as a manufacturing center of Indian jewelry (Figs. 60–63). Many businesses have set up shop employing silversmiths and inlayers to produce their line of jewelry (Fig. 64). Piecework may also be given out to silversmiths who are supplied with materials to work into finished pieces at home. Almost all of this work is done by Navajos (Fig. 65). Only a few Zunis participate in this system. The manufacturer's task is to produce as much jewelry that fits the criterion of "authentic, handmade" as possible, as cheaply as possible, but also with as much artistry and style as this market allows. Zuni craftsmen are happy to take orders but have not taken to working set hours at a place away from Zuni, nor to working for someone else who dictates the work to be done.

Figure 60. Dowtown Gallup, Route 66

The Gallup Ceremonial, known throughout
the country as a meeting for Indian performers,
craftsmen, and traders, has more recently begun to
reflect the attitude of a town which is the center
of Indian jewelry manufacture than a place where
Indian jewelry is traded. The consequences of this
are twofold: Indian arts are seen more as
commodities than as art and cultural differences
do not weigh heavily.

Prizes are awarded at the ceremonial for pieces
entered into competition. Outside judges are
brought in to mediate, and ribbons and cash
prizes are awarded. Winning an award is an
important step for a craftsman and has market
consequences. For the most part, categories for
judging follow types, not cultural distinctions.
That is, jewelry is categorized by the type of
work—inlay, needlepoint, cluster—rather than by
tribe. Pottery is categorized by size and function

Figure 61. Plywood tepees at east end store, Gallup

Figure 62. Awning of trader's store, Gallup

49

Figure 63. Outside display at Gallup trader's store

Figure 64. Request for inlayers, Gallup

rather than by tribe (except that a new category has been added for Navajo pottery). The net effect of cultural impartiality, interestingly, has been to reduce Zuni participation and to make the ceremonial more of a Navajo show. Judges are more impressed by size, color, innovation, and precious stones than they are by how these objects exemplify the best in separate cultural traditions. The upshot is that Zuni artists feel that the subtlety and exactness of their work has been overshadowed in the judges' minds by more showy Navajo work. For example, the 1994 Gallup Ceremonial Premium Book lists 347 categories for awarding prizes. While submissions require proof of tribal affiliation, four-fifths of them specify no particular tribe or cultural identity. The remaining fifth, however, specifies that the pieces to be entered are Navajo, with token amounts given to Ute/Paiute, Pueblo,

Figure 65. Manufacturer's work area, Gallup

Papago, Hopi, Apache, and Northwest Coast. It is noteworthy that no category lists Zuni as a cultural distinction.

The Museum of Northern Arizona, on the other hand, produces shows which maintain cultural identities and has a long tradition of producing a Navajo and Hopi show; in 1987 the museum initiated a Zuni show. Zuni craftsmen responded very favorably to this show, submitting their work and attending the openings. They participated because there were prizes and prize money and because it was a celebration of Zuni culture and arts. The net effect of the Museum of Northern Arizona show has been to distinguish new work and to catapult new Zuni artists to the forefront of Native American arts.

The other notable market which has an impact on Zuni work is the Santa Fe Indian Market. This show is juried and artists submit slides of their work for review by a panel. If the artist is accepted, he is allowed to sell his or her work in a ten-foot-square booth on the Plaza or along an adjacent street on an August weekend. Collectors gather in Santa Fe for Indian Market weekend, (all hotels are reserved a year in advance) and line up before dawn to be the first in line to buy from a craftsman. Prizewinners sell first. Though Zunis are underrepresented—perhaps twelve out of 250 booths are Zuni—the market is an excellent showcase for those Zunis that participate, and an opportunity to directly cultivate retail buyers and to take orders for additional work. While some judging categories make cultural distinctions and others do not, within the booths the craftsmen sell only their own and their families' work; cultural distinctions are clearly maintained within their ten square feet.

PART III

HISTORIC AND CONTEMPORARY JEWELRY

BY MARIAN RODEE

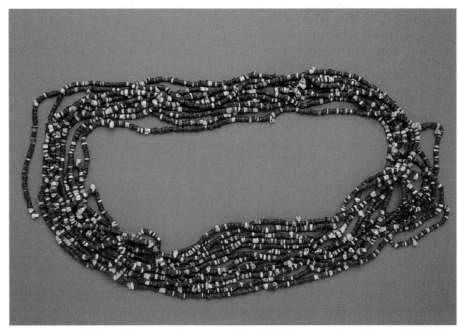

THE ZUNIS AND THEIR ANCESTORS HAVE BEEN MAKING JEWELRY FOR OVER ONE THOUSAND YEARS. IN PREHISTORIC TIMES THERE WERE SEVERAL REGIONAL CULTURE AREAS IN THE SOUTHWEST, EACH WITH ITS OWN STYLE OF JEWELRY. THE ZUNI REGION IS IN THE ANASAZI AND MOGOLLON CULTURE AREA WHERE ANCIENT ORNAMENTS WERE CARVED AND DRILLED FROM SHELL, TURQUOISE, AND OTHER STONES. ALTHOUGH METAL WORKING WAS NOT PRACTICED UNTIL THE ARRIVAL OF THE SPANISH, SMALL COPPER BELLS WERE TRADED PREHISTORICALLY FROM MEXICO WHERE THERE WAS A METAL WORKING INDUSTRY AND THERE IS EVIDENCE THAT THEY WERE STRUNG WITH LOCALLY MADE BEADS IN JEWELRY (JERNIGAN 1978, 74).

Many of the forms of jewelry did not change over the centuries; indeed some pieces made and worn today are almost identical to those found in early sites scattered throughout the region (Fig. 66). Fine disc beads, popularly called *heishe* from the Keresan word for shell bead, along with tab or rectangular pendants are still popular, although no longer made at Zuni. Beads are still produced at Santo Domingo, however, and traders from there supply many Zuni jewelers today. Two of the more contemporary artists, Carlton Jamon and Veronica Poblano, are learning to make beads from Andy Kirk of Isleta Pueblo.

Some of the most impressive ancient jewelry comes from the archaeological sites at Chaco Canyon, especially from Pueblo Bonito where over 56,000 pieces of turquoise were recovered from one room in the 1890s excavations by George Pepper (Windes 1992, 159). A small site near Fajada Butte in Chaco Canyon (29SJ629), dating from the late A.D. 900s to early 1000s, contained thousands of bits of turquoise, chips, and beads broken in drilling, but only one finished bead. These finds indicate that the inhabitants of this small village specialized in making turquoise beads which were then apparently traded to the larger ceremonial centers such as Pueblo Bonito where they have been found in kivas and shrines (Windes 1992, 160).

Although Chaco Canyon sites indicate that the villages in this area were a center of turquoise use and production during the Pueblo II and perhaps Pueblo III periods, there is no source of the raw material in the canyon. The well-known mines in

Figure 66. Necklace, Pueblo Bonito. National Museum of Natural History

Top: Figure 67. Jet bird pendant, *Hawikku*. National Museum of the American Indian

53

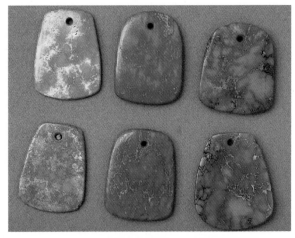

Figure 68. Six tab pendants, Pueblo Bonito.
National Museum of Natural History

Figure 69. Sandstone saws, Pueblo Bonito.
National Museum of Natural History

Figure 70. Abrader, Pueblo Bonito.
National Museum of Natural History

Cerrillos, New Mexico, just south of Santa Fe, are a possible source. A few mine pits there are accompanied by pottery made in the Chaco area, indicating a trading connection or at least that people from Chaco came to the Cerrillos area to dig a supply of turquoise. There is a myth among the Zuni that there were mines in the Zuni Mountains, although they have never been identified. The Zuni belief was that Turquoise Boy was offended by the Zuni people and fled the area. This may indicate an abandonment or playing out of the mines near Zuni. Some suggest Mount Sedgewick in this range may have been the ancient site of the mines since related resources such and copper and silver are found there today (Windes 1992, 163). Mineralogical analysis of ancient turquoise has not determined the source of the raw materials.

Although the forms of prehistoric jewelry are relatively simple, the amount of work involved in creating such pieces is immense, especially considering the craftsmen had only stone, bone, and wood tools. Sandstone saws and abraders for smoothing and polishing pieces were also found at Pueblo Bonito, as well as a piece of turquoise partially sawn from the matrix (Figs. 69–72). The ability of the early artists is evident in the way the small cut pieces are fitted into a harmonious pattern (Fig. 74). In some instances a particularly fine drilled bead is used in a new inlay plaque (Fig. 73). In most cases the backing is wood, but occasionally shell is utilized, the traditional glue being pitch or wax. Clearly, considerable time was required for all this cutting with only simple stone-tipped drills rotated between the hands. The other site representative of prehistoric Zuni jewelry is Hawikku (Hawikuh). Hawikku is one of the fabled Seven Cities of Cibola which was supposedly filled with gold and silver and contained houses ornamented with turquoise. These supposed wonders were reported by Alvar Nuñes Cabeza de Vaca and his two companions who were shipwrecked off the coast of Florida and made their way cross-country until they reached Mexico City

Figure 71. Abrader, Pueblo Bonito.
National Museum of Natural History

Figure 72. Turquoise partially cut from matrix,
Pueblo Bonito. National Museum of Natural History

Figure 73. Turquoise mosaic plaques, *Hawikku*. Pueblo IV.
National Museum of the American Indian

Left: Figure 74. Inlaid blade,
Poncho House Ruin, Arizona. Pueblo III.
Peabody Museum of Archaeology
and Ethnology, Harvard University.
Photograph by Hillel Burger

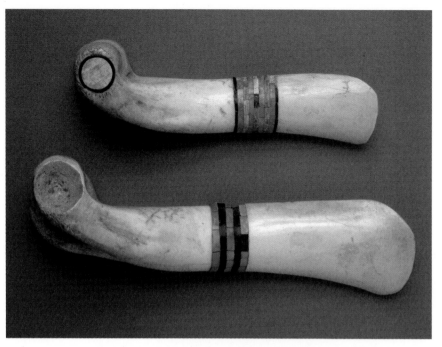

Figure 75. Inlaid deer bone scrapers, Pueblo Bonito. National Museum of Natural History

Figure 76. Jet lizard pendant, Pueblo Bonito. National Museum of Natural History

Figure 77. Jet insect pendant, Pueblo Bonito. National Museum of Natural History

Figure 78. Turquoise bird pendant, Pueblo Bonito. National Museum of Natural History

in 1536. Their tales of gold and turquoise riches inspired an expedition in 1539 led by the Franciscan father Marcos de Niza and the Moor Estevan who had traveled with Cabeza de Vaca. Estevan entered *Hawikku* (or possibly *Kyaki:ma*) first and was killed apparently for some insult or arrogant act. Father Marcos, fearing to enter the village, only observed it from a distance. The following year a military party led by Francisco Vásquez Coronado fought a battle at *Hawikku* and captured the town. A mission church was begun in *Hawikku*, one of the villages along the Zuni River, in 1629. The mission was destroyed in the Pueblo rebellion of 1680 and never rebuilt. *Hawikku* was occupied from about A.D. 1300 to 1680.

The most distinctive pieces of jewelry found at *Hawikku* are wooden combs, their ends covered with turquoise inlays and occasional touches of jet. Carved in one piece with a variable number of teeth, the smallest comb measures 3 1/4" with the mosaic 1 1/16" wide by 11/16" long. These were worn thrust into the woman's hair which had been knotted at the back of the head (Hodge 1921, 18–19).

The southern neighbors of the Zunis, who went to their region to trade for buffalo hides and turquoise, told the Spanish that the Zunis wore turquoise in their ears and noses. This may be an interpreter's error since body piercing was not a common Anasazi practice (except for the ear lobes). Only one possible nose ornament has been found in the Anasazi region (Jernigan 1978, Fig. 78). When the Spanish travelers visited Zuni themselves they made no mention of such nose ornaments, only turquoise necklaces and earrings.

There is no evidence as to the style of jewelry produced at Zuni during the eighteenth and early nineteenth centuries. Presumably it had changed little except for the addition of a few glass and metal beads and pendants. The Sitgreaves Expedition of 1853 observed a blacksmith shop operating at Zuni and Plate 5 in the report by Richard Kern, the expedition illustrator, shows two men at work in the shop, one at a bellows and the other at an anvil (Sitgreaves 1853, Pl. 5).

More solid information on the pueblo is recorded by the anthropologists on the three Smithsonian Institution expeditions beginning in 1879. The expedition's photographer, John Hillers, did many portraits of men and women adorned in their best clothes and jewelry (Fig. 3). These show that in addition to the ancient-style turquoise and shell ornaments, silver necklaces, buttons, and bracelets in the Navajo style were also worn.

When John Adair was doing his fieldwork at Zuni in 1937 and 1938, he extensively interviewed the first silversmith of the village, La:niyadhi (Lanyade), who was then about ninety-five (Adair 1944, 122–130). Around 1872, the Navajo silversmith, Atsidi Chon (Ugly Smith), a friend and trading partner of La:niyahdi, came to live with him at Zuni. Atsidi Chon made silver jewelry for the Zunis, but kept himself locked up in La:niyahdi's house so no one could see how he worked. For the payment of a horse Atsidi Chon taught La:niyahdi silversmithing. He also taught him to make dies or stamps out of iron to decorate the silver for the Zuni men who worked copper and brass jewelry and who had only used files for this purpose (Figs. 79 and 80).

La:niyahdi kept his work secret for a while, so that he could make more money by being the only silversmith in the village and, in the last quarter of the nineteenth century, in the whole area south

Figure 79. Silver and brass bracelets. Late nineteenth century. National Museum of Natural History

Figure 80. Brass rings. Late nineteenth century. National Museum of the American Indian

Top: Figure 81. La:niyahdi's hammer. Late nineteenth century. National Museum of Natural History

Figure 84. La:niyahdi's ceramic crucible.
Late nineteenth century.
National Museum of Natural HIstory

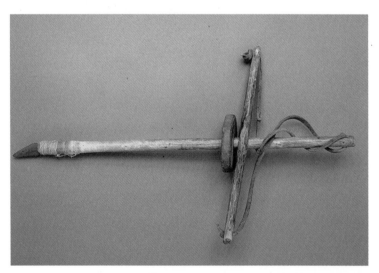

Figure 83. La:niyahdi's bow drill. Late nineteenth century.
National Museum of Natural History

Above: Figure 82. La:niyahdi's metal crucible.
Late nineteenth century.
National Museum of Natural History

of Gallup. La:niyahdi later taught his friend Balawade to make silver. Both of these men made silver jewelry for anthropologist Frank Cushing during his stay at Zuni, including all the buttons on his trousers and his concha belts ($12 each belt). Balawade taught other older men the craft. They were Yachilthle, Lawiaocelo, Hacecenane, Kiwianade, and Kwaisedemon. Matilda Coxe Stevenson bought La:niyahdi's tools for $50 before she left the pueblo for the last time in 1902. Figures 81–88 show all of the tools, except for several of his ceramic crucibles. La:niyahdi didn't make much silver after his tools were bought for the Smithsonian, so that subsequently most people in the village did not realize he had been the first Zuni to make silver jewelry.

An early item of male adornment is the bowguard, in its simplest form a leather band worn on the wrist to protect it from the snap of the released bowstring. Some early bowguards were ornamented with "tin," that is, tinned sheet

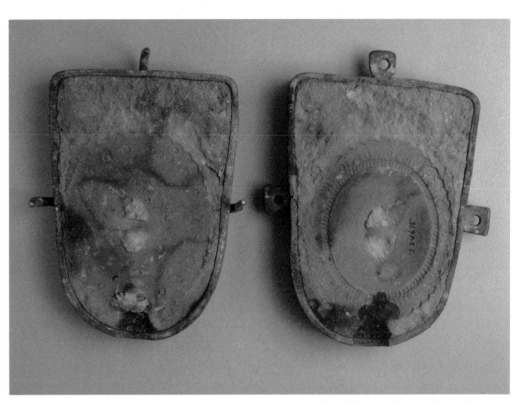

Figure 85. La:niyahdi's mold for concha. Late nineteenth century.
National Museum of Natural History

Right: Figure 86. La:niyahdi's cloth-wrapped blowpipe.
Late nineteenth century.
National Museum of Natural History

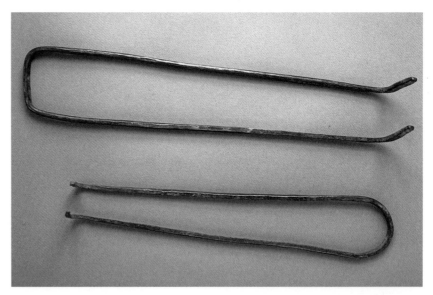

Figure 88. La:niyahdi's pincers. Late nineteenth century.
National Museum of Natural History

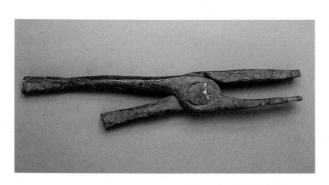

Figure 87. La:niyahdi's tongs.
Late nineteenth century.
National Museum of Natural History

iron (Fig. 89) in cut-out floral designs, and the first silver ones use the same technique in the same patterns (Fig. 90).

Late nineteenth-century Zuni silversmithing looks much like that of the Navajo—the same buttons, beads, silver hoop earrings, and bracelets. This is partially because they were buying them from Navajo smiths and because the first Zuni smiths learned their techniques and patterns from Navajos. The National Museum of the American Indian owns a collection of jewelry purchased from Douglas Graham who operated a trading post at Zuni from 1881 to 1898 and was also the agent for the U.S. government in Zuni from 1880 to 1885. The collection notes do not indicate whether they are pieces that were made at the pueblo or material Graham was trading to them. In any event, the jewelry probably represents the popular taste in ornaments at the pueblo at the end of the nineteenth century. These styles were common as well among most of the tribes of the Southern Plains. Bracelets were worn by both men and women—simple wire bracelets decorated with a few chisel marks

Figure 89. Tinned bowguards. Late nineteenth century.
National Museum of Natural History

Figure 90. Silver bowguard. Late nineteenth century.
National Museum of the American Indian

and of brass or German silver, sometimes of silver. The ones with elaborately stamped patterns are more characteristic of the early twentieth-century Navajo style (Fig. 91).

The tools of La:niyahdi's set show what early workers were capable of. The numerous crucibles in the set are made of ceramic and iron and, since sheet sterling was unavailable, all silver was melted down from coins—first American and later the common Mexican peso—after which the metal was hammered into the desired shapes. Wire of varying diameters would be made by pulling silver through the holes of a drawplate. No stamps in the set indicate the style of the period.

The Zunis did not set stones into silver jewelry until around 1890 (Adair 1944, 128). At first there were only a few small stones in rings and bracelets, but as the twentieth century advanced more turquoise was available to the artists and the traditional Zuni love of stones reasserted itself.

Figure 91. Silver bracelets with elaborate stamps.
c. 1900. National Museum of the American Indian

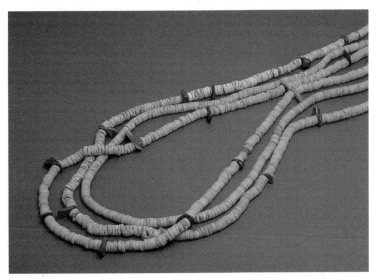

Figure 92. *Heishe* necklace.
National Museum of the American Indian

Figure 93. Silver bracelets. Late nineteenth century.
National Museum of the American Indian

Figure 94. Horn and bone necklace. c. 1900
National Museum of the American Indian

Figure 95. Turquoise mosaic necklace
based on *Hawikku* pottery
design by Frank Vacit.
The Heard Museum

Figure 96. Turquoise squash
blossom necklace
by Warren and Doris Ondelacy.
Private collection

Figure 97. Turquoise and coral
squash blossom necklace
by Dan Simplicio, 1945.
The Heard Museum

When the trader C.G. Wallace set up business in the pueblo in 1917, he said there were only five Zuni silversmiths there. He soon employed local Navajos to set Zuni-cut stones. For a number of years Zunis glued the sets of cut stones to cardboard backings and sold them to traders who in turn passed the premounted sets on to Navajo silversmiths. The trade worked both ways, with silver backs made for sale to the Zunis, and this arrangement proved to be profitable for both groups. The majority of pieces set in this way were Rainbow Man and Knifewing figures, and often two jewelers would "collaborate" on a piece without ever having met (Neumann 1950, 175).

Changes after World War II, beginning in the late 1940s, brought technological improvements which led to stylistic changes. Gasoline blow torches were introduced, making greater control of solder possible, which in turn meant that jewelry consisting of smaller stones in more delicate settings could be made. The traders also began carrying lighter gauge silver for bezels. These developments led to elaborate and complex patterns often on an expanded scale. In 1950 electricity was brought into the village, enabling use of motor-driven wheels and diamond-tooth saws (Neumann 1950, 174).

Around 1912, F.A. Marcher of Los Angeles opened turquoise mines in Nevada, had the stones cut, and made an annual sales trip across the Southwestern reservations. In 1915, Paul Kley of Denver also began making Nevada turquoise available. It is only since 1915 that good quality turquoise has been readily available in the Southwest (Kirk 1945, 31). The turquoise most frequently used in Zuni at mid-century was Lone Mountain and Battle Mountain, both from Nevada (Neumann 1950, 177). During the war, jewelers were forced to use low-grade soft turquoise from the Arizona copper mine region.

Around 1930, when the Mexican government banned the export of silver pesos, Mike Kirk of

Kirk Brothers, traders at Gallup and Zuni, sent an old coin to a smelter to have it copied, but they ended up producing a one-ounce square slug (Kirk 1945, 45). Silversmiths were in the habit of throwing a certain number of coins in a crucible to melt for a particular piece, so it was a matter of convenience in working, rather than any preference in silver content, that made smiths chose coins. The silver content of all pre-1905 Mexican silver coinage was of .903 fineness, American coins were .900, and sterling is .925, all of it alloyed with copper and hence of little practical difference. There was also a shortage of silver during World War II and some otherwise excellent pieces were set on aluminum (Fig. 137). After the war, as noted previously, more commercial sheet and wire silver was available at the pueblo.

Another innovation of the Kirks resulted in a special order of mosaic jewelry made for archaeologist Frederick W. Hodge and inspired by the ancient mosaic work found at Hawikku. Teddy Weahkee (Meahkie) did the stonework for the piece but there is no description of what the pattern was. C.G. Wallace, a long-time trader in Zuni, had a necklace made by Frank Vacit for his wife based on Hawikku pottery designs (Fig. 95). After that, Kirk said that other artists began to make mosaics of Rainbow God and Knifewing (Kirk 1945, 43) (Fig. 146).

By the middle of this century the style most associated with the Zuni was well established. Called clusterwork, it consists of a mass of stones arranged in a flowerlike pattern resembling a design on their ceramic water jars (Fig. 120). Over the years this clusterwork has become increasingly finer, and some stones are so small that they must be mounted on toothpicks to set. By 1950 most of the silver jewelry worn by the Navajo themselves was Zuni-made and of the cluster style. Although the Navajo Guild promoted heavy silver pieces in the older simpler style of the late nineteenth century (as they do to this day), they were usually purchased by collectors rather than by the Navajo themselves.

In 1935 Congress created the Indian Arts and Crafts Board with John Collier, the Commissioner of Indian Affairs, as its Chairman. E.K. Burlew, Assistant Secretary of the Interior, Dr. A.V. Kidder, Lorenzo Hubbell, Jr., James W. Young, and Rene d'Harnoncourt were its original members. Prominent art historian d'Harnoncourt in 1941 organized the second major museum exhibit of Native American art (exclusive of world's fairs and other international expositions). The venue of this historically important show was significant—the Museum of Modern Art, New York City, the capital of American art (Department of Interior, 1941). The Board was very distinguished, but the only Indian trader on it was Lorenzo Hubbell, Jr., son of the famous Lorenzo Hubbell of Ganado, Arizona.

The goals of the Board were to promote Indian art and to secure more money for its makers. The method was to mark pieces of the highest quality. "The Board has reached the conclusion that the Government mark should be applied only to the finest quality of wholly genuine, truly hand-fashioned and authentic Indian silver and turquoise products" (Collier, 1937). Machine-produced curio jewelry, then as now, was a problem for traditional artists. Reproduced here are the government standards (Collier, 1937):

1. Material. Silver slugs of 1 ounce weight or other silver objects may be used, provided their fineness is at least 900; and provided further, that no silver sheet shall be used. Unless cast, the slug or other object is to be hand hammered to thickness and shape desired. The only exceptions here are pins on brooches or similar objects; ear screws for earrings; backs for tie clasps and chain, which may be of silver of different fineness and mechanically made.

2. Dies. Dies used are to be entirely hand-made, with no tool more mechanical than hand tools and vice. Dies shall contain only a single element of the design.

3. Application of dies. Dies are to be applied to the object with the aid of nothing except hand tools.

4. Appliqué elements in design. All such parts of the ornament are to be hand-made. If wire is used, it is to be hand-made with no tool other than a hand-made draw plate. These requirements apply to the boxes for stones used in the design.

5. Stone for ornamentation. In addition to turquoise, the use of other local stone is permitted. Turquoise, if used, must be genuine stone, uncolored by any artificial means.

6. Cutting of stone. All stone used, including turquoise, is to be hand-cut and polished. This permits the use of hand or foot-driven wheels.

7. Finish. All silver is to be hand polished.

Of course no power-driven machinery was permitted. An addendum to these standards, written by Kenneth M. Chapman of the Laboratory of Anthropology in Santa Fe, stated, "Gasoline and acetylene torches are permitted, since any industrious smith can acquire one, and their use does not in any way affect the quality or appearance of the finished product." These rather exalted standards came at a time when numerous shortcuts in the forms of power tools, sheet silver, and commercial wire were becoming more available. The board was fighting a losing battle, however, since most artists wanted to use faster and better tools and equipment. The sole official stamp was in the care of Kenneth Chapman and the staff of the Laboratory of Anthropology. This meant that the pieces had to be shipped to Chapman or he had to make periodic visits to the reservations to examine and approve jewelry. Chapman even had a gauge that measured the thickness of the silver so that he could tell whether its uniformity denoted sheet or handmade silver.

Writing to Margaret McKittrick of the American Association on Indian Affairs in New York City on May 11, 1938, Chapman stated that he had examined about four thousand pieces of silver of which about half were approved and stamped. This material had been held for many months for Chapman to inspect and was subsequently sent to the National Parks for sale, since the Department of Interior ran both Indian Affairs and the Park Service. His dies read U.S. Navajo, U.S. Zuni, and U.S. Hopi with the maker's, trader's, or wholesaler's number. A special stamp, which he does not describe, was necessary for most Zuni pieces because of the amount of turquoise. Chapman said the turquoise was of poor quality because jewelers were not able to find good stones. He only vouched for the fact it was handcut. He ended with, "Most of the plain silver is of a very high quality, but unfortunately the preference is for that with turquoise" (Chapman, 1938). Chapman also loaned the dies to knowledgeable judges to mark silver. For instance, in a letter of March 25, 1940, to H. Bogard, Superintendent of Fort Wingate Vocational School, Chapman said he sent the stamps to Ambrose Roanhorse and Dooley Shorty to stamp work by their students.

In a letter dated March 8, 1939, trader C.G. Wallace wrote to Kenneth Chapman for help. "May I ask that you help me make one more effort before I have to give up the ship as to the stamped jewelry?" (He was referring to the government stamp.) Wallace wanted the government to do something about the traders in Zuni.

"Some of the Traders here in Zuni have always fought the idea and are still doing everything within their power to keep the Indians from making the jewelry that would take the stamp and of course the Indian seeks the easiest way. These same Traders by use of rollers and sheet silver have been selling plain silver for less than one dollar per ounce." (Chapman Papers)

Wallace also sought support to keep the National Parks and Fred Harvey Co. from selling so much "rolled" jewelry, which seems to be a term for any manufactured work.

The Indian Arts and Crafts Board did not have the manpower to enforce these difficult standards and mark all the eligible pieces. Dealers could not afford to keep pieces off the market for months while waiting for the work to be stamped in order to comply with the new standards. The Board was fighting a losing battle against modernization of the craft. There is also something quite paternalistic about the government trying to preserve archaic techniques in the work of their "wards." Chapman's previously quoted comment —"but unfortunately the preference is for that [jewelry] with turquoise" —shows the aesthetic preference of the Anglos who wrote the arts and crafts regulations, although it is quite evident that both Zuni and Navajo tastes ran to multiple turquoise settings. Also, it is doubtful whether Anglo-American jewelers were drawing their own wire and hammering pieces from slugs. The program was gradually abandoned and the newly formed Navajo and Hopi arts and crafts guilds took up the practice of marking jewelry.

Figure 98. Thelma Sheche and granddaughters

"Getting all painted" up is the translation for a Zuni phrase that means to get dressed up for a dance or ceremony. When asked what the ideal set of jewelry was, a Zuni woman laughed and said, "As much as you have. Rings on every finger, earrings, as many bracelets that will fit, with or without comfort, on the arms and two or three necklaces" (Fig. 98). In the old photos both men and women are shown wearing multiple necklaces. The true ideal is a traditional black handwoven manta or dress with as many large clusterwork pins going down the right side as it is possible to fit. These manta pins are especially characteristic of Zuni (Fig. 100).

In the work environment only a small amount of jewelry is worn, perhaps a discreet ring, bracelet, or pin/pendant. In a probably unrelated trend, many modern Anglo women also seem to feel that too much jewelry at work is unprofessional. Jewelry is a popular gift for graduates just as tiny bracelets are given to babies. Jewelry is a valuable possession of the family, and many keep a collection of jewelry that belongs to the house or matrilineage and is not to be sold (Figs. 43–46). However, individuals are generous in lending jewelry to those family members and friends who need it for a ceremony or for decorating a *Sha'lak'o* house.

Warrior kachinas usually wear silver and turquoise bowguards as well as the ancient style of shell and turquoise bead necklaces. Even objects such as mountain lion skin quivers will have bowguards or manta pins attached (Fig.102). Duane Quam, husband of Alice Quam, made himself a handsome silver and turquoise tomahawk for the Comanche Dance, of which he was the chief at one time (Fig.101). While women may wear as much jewelry as they can carry, a man who is taking part in a kachina dance must be more restrained. At one dance a man wore many bright new silver and turquoise pins on his kilt and was criticized for being too flashy. While the more modern styles are appreciated and worn, the older cluster style is preferred for getting painted up. The stores at the pueblo will display lighter, more modern jewelry during the summer tourist season, but in the fall as *Sha'la'ko* and all the other important traditional activities of the season approach, more cluster jewelry is displayed and sold.

For traditional historic reasons turquoise is the most popular stone for jewelry, followed by shells of various types; now there are more exotic shells then ever before available through the international trade. The preferred turquoise is clear sky blue with little or no matrix or inclusions. Green will be used on special order, but most Zuni people do not like it for their own jewelry. Coral is still used and valued, but it is getting more expensive and the pieces are smaller with more holes in the branches—making it more difficult to work with.

Quality of materials is an important aesthetic consideration. Silver should be of medium gauge, neither too heavy nor too light, combined with good quality, well-matched stones. This is more difficult than it sounds. In one single shell, for instance, a wide range of tones often occurs naturally. The stones cut from one large nugget of turquoise will match, but perhaps not from another chunk from the same mine.

Equally important in Zuni aesthetics as the materials, perhaps even more so, is the level of workmanship. All Zunis seem to understand and appreciate fine craftsmanship. They will look at a piece slowly, bending over it or bringing it up close. Sets must be even and the stones must fit perfectly—no corners cut off and filled in with silver where it does not meet the bezel or housing. Good workmanship is not just visual but tactile, and the quality of finish and polish can be felt as much as seen. The artists who work in the silver

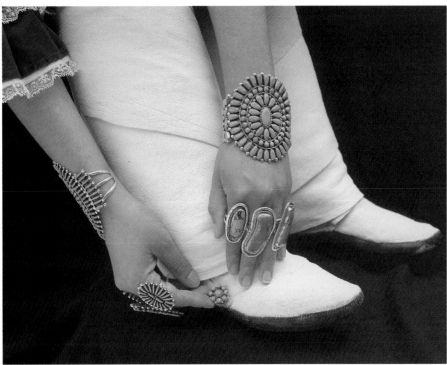

Figure 99. Miss Zuni, Brenda Harker, fastening her moccasins

Figure 100. Manta with pins by Lorraine Quam Waatsa

inlay style put such a high polish on their silver that it reflects light like a mirror and hence is quite difficult to photograph.

As in the other arts, learning is a family process. Children help with small chores around the workbench, including polishing and sorting. As they grow older they learn more of the art from their parents. Women usually do the stone setting and men the silverwork. This is said to be because women have smaller, more delicate fingers for setting and cutting. In the past, very few women

Figure 101. Comanche Dance tomahawk by Duane Quam

did silverwork, but since the 1950s, when electricity and power tools became common in the village, more women have taken up the working of the metal as well. The general availability of wire and sheet silver also was a factor in eliminating the more strenuous part of silverwork.

Although families may share a common style, frequently there are small design gestures that define individuality. For instance, in the Edaakie family, Dennis, the father, is now making inlay jewelry featuring the Rio Grande clown or Koshare. Dennis's Koshare wear moccasins, but those of his two sons, Myron and Derrick, wear tennis shoes. In another family, the Soseeahs, the eldest daughter, Burdian, makes Sun Face jewelry set with turquoise; her younger sister, Denise, does half a sun face set with mother of pearl; and the youngest sister does a half sun face set with shell and dangles. This type of division may only be apparent within the village, but it gives each artist a specialty within the more recognizable family style.

Families may also develop a style which proves to be very popular and then becomes driven by the marketplace. Dealers will ask for more and more of a particular type of ring or bracelet that sells well and the artist may make literally hundreds of them. This can be difficult for a creative individual, and one artist told me that he will repeat a style for a while because he has large orders to fill, but then will introduce a small change or two to keep his design sense fresh and yet still provide an income.

Figure 102. Bowguards by Alice Quam on mountain lion quiver

NUGGET STYLE

WHEN ZUNIS SPEAK OF STYLE THEY ARE
REALLY TALKING ABOUT TECHNIQUE;
THEREFORE THE FOLLOWING DISCUSSION
WILL CATEGORIZE ARTISTS IN TERMS OF
THE TECHNIQUE THEY EMPLOY. NUGGET
STYLE IS RELATED TO THE NAVAJO
STYLE OF JEWELRY WITH HEAVY
STAMPED SILVERWORK AND MASSIVE
SINGLE STONES.

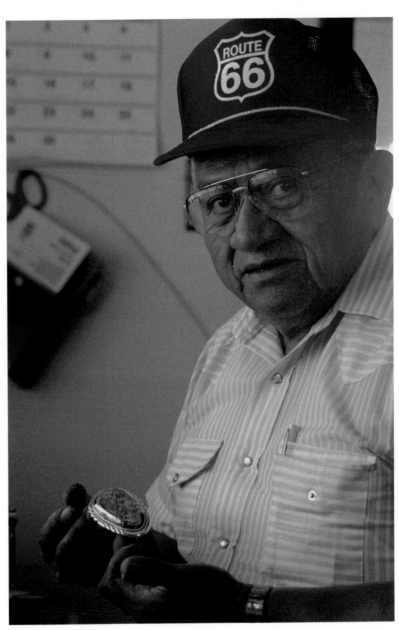

Figure 104. Robert Leekya holding a finished buckle

Figure 103. Robert Leekya cutting a bezel

Figure 105. Buckle by Robert Leekya

Figure 106. Watchband by Robert Leekya

BERNICE AND ROBERT LEEKYA

One of the leading families employing this style is that of Bernice and Robert Leekya (Figs. 108–112). Robert learned from his father, Leekya Deyuse, who was perhaps more famous as a stone cutter and fetish carver than a silversmith. Robert says he was the first to work in this style about 1953. However, the family of Dan Simplicio believes that Dan was working in the nugget style in the 1940s (see Fig. 102) and taught his brothers, Kirk and Chauncey. Although Navajos use precut stones, Robert and Bernice are proud of

the fact that they cut their own stones and use only the best quality Sleeping Beauty turquoise that has not been treated in any way, even with plastic backings. (Many turquoise sets are backed with black plastic which cushions the stone, making it easier to set and also making it appear deeper than it really is.)

Leekya family work only uses a small piece of tissue paper as a backing because they feel that plastic changes the color. Bernice and Robert believe they are the only ones doing this style at the pueblo, although his sister Sarah does nugget necklaces (not set in silver). His sisters, Sarah and Alice (who is now deceased), married two brothers, Lambert and Bernard Homer. Robert has two brothers, Roger and Frances, who do channelwork.

The Leekyas have a beautifully equipped detached studio with good light. They work side by side in front of large windows that look out on Blackrock. The anvil is placed on top of an old tree stump which Robert obtained in Oklahoma. This raises the anvil to a good working height and absorbs the blows from his hammer. Bernice learned cluster-work from her family, the Quams, in the evenings during the 1940s. She stopped working in this style when she married Robert. In the 1960s they made mosaic Knifewings and Rainbow Men and often attended shows, but have become too busy with dealers' orders and now only enter the Gallup Ceremonial.

The Leekyas believe their work is popular because of the high quality of the stones they use and the heaviness of their silver (18–26 gauge), even for the bezels because it holds the stones more securely. They only work in turquoise, coral, white shell, and jet though they used to work in gold before the price rose so high. Because of all their orders they try to keep a strict work schedule of 7 A.M. to 5 P.M. that is unusual for most Zuni craftspeople. Their children do not live at the pueblo and are not jewelers, so the continuity of the family style is in some doubt.

CASTING

CASTING IS ONE OF THE OLDEST TECHNIQUES OF SILVERWORKERS AT THE PUEBLO, AS CAN BE SEEN IN LA:NIYAHDI'S TOOL SET WITH ITS CRUCIBLES AND MOLD.

THE IULE FAMILY

The most famous family of jewelers who work in the casting style is that of the children of Horace Iule. During his research in the late 1930s and again in 1978, John Adair stayed with Horace and wrote about him (Adair 1944, 137–143). Horace Iule learned blacksmithing at the Phoenix Indian School and then became a silversmith, eventually teaching the subject at the Zuni Day School (Fig. 108). Lupe Iule, Horace's daughter, and her husband George Leekity live in the family home and continue the tradition of casting (Fig. 107). George carves patterns for his own original jewelry out of plywood (Fig. 109). After being cast they are stamped G & L Leekity, but they stamp Iule on pieces using Horace's designs. Lupe, now forty-one, worked with her father from the time she was thirteen. She married in 1970 and her husband George learned from Horace around 1972. George remembers that

Figure 107. Lupe Iule and George Leekity

Figure 108. Horace Iule and his class at Zuni Day School, c. 1920. University of New Mexico, Maxwell Museum of Anthroplogy

73

Figure 109. Wood patterns

Figure 110. Heating silver in a crucible

Figure 111. Getting ready to pour silver

Horace drew his patterns on a stone, carved them out, and then poured silver in the stone. This process is like the twentieth-century Navajo method. The family buys scrap silver from other silversmiths and then melts it up for casting. The molds are made from river sand, Portland cement, and oil which George mixes himself. Since an original Iule piece is pressed into the mold and then cast, the contemporary buyer is getting his exact design each time. This process is identical to that used by La:niyahdi for making the mold of a concho (Fig. 85). The filler is knocked out, remixed, and another piece pressed into the mold. Larger pieces require larger crucibles, such as a fruit can, or a charcoal forge for really big pieces. A large ten-inch cross requires thirteen ounces of silver.

Lupe's brothers, Barney and Philip, also do castings as does her daughter Rosella. Her sisters, Ruby and Cecilia, do not cast; they have office jobs in the pueblo but do finishing work, such as polishing and setting stones, in the evenings. The whole family used to work together before Horace died. In the summer Lupe and George start work at 4:30 A.M. to avoid the heat of the day. The Iules have done special orders, including one large cross for a bishop in Paris that had to be cast in three parts and joined.

Figure 112. Crosses ready to be set

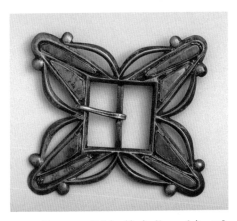

Figure 114. Belt buckle by Horace Iule, 1928.
The Heard Museum

Figure 113. Finished crosses

Figure 115. Cast Knifewing squash blossom necklace
by Juan Dedios, 1930. The Heard Museum

Figure 116. Clark and Bessie Couyancy

CLARK COUYANCY

Until Clark Couyancy stopped making silver in 1990 he was for many years perhaps the most outstanding jeweler to work in this older style (Figs. 117 and 118). Clark was born in 1908 but it was not until 1945 that he learned silver-smithing from his brother Franklin. At that time he hammered out Mexican pesos into bracelets and employed square-cut stone sets. Using a triangular file on pieces of silver and brass, he added borax to produce solder and melted the mixture with a blowtorch. He cleaned his silver with water and a homemade

Figure 117. Three-row bracelet by Clark Couyancy

acid made from a saltlike crystal (*ma:ts'a*) he found near Ojo Caliente (see Charles Hustito, p. 116). His turquoise sets were squared off by cutting and grinding them on a hand-operated wheel, with sandpaper used for the final finish. In 1955 he gave up the *ma:ts'a* and poured acid out of old batteries, heated the bracelets, and immersed them. Next he laid out all the turquoise sets to be considered and matched them. He didn't know what kind of turquoise it was because his wife Bessie bought it for him. In fact she and her sister, Emma Ketsinik, set the stones for him and he shared his profits with them.

In 1950 Clark bought a motor and an acetylene torch. He also used a drawplate to make his own wire and didn't start buying 8 gauge commercial wire until 1956. With the torch and motor it was easier to make the silver bracelets—he worked the wire into the desired shape and used 32 gauge strips for the housings and drops with a snakelike stamp for terminal decorations.

When he started making row bracelets in 1945 he initially received $2 a row, then $3, and then $5 from the Kirk Brothers until he finally ended up receiving $10 per row. Since it had become easier to make bracelets out of wire he decided to add more rows to the bracelet, each of them attached by soldered drops. The technique of using drops of solder to hold bracelet components together was his idea. He charged $20 per row for up to ten rows. The process of making such pieces was still very laborious. A White lady came to order two bracelets, one ten-row and the other fifteen, it took him three weeks to complete the order.

ELEANOR AHIYITE

Eleanor says she is sixty-five or sixty-seven years old and learned row work from her brother Wallace when she was about twenty-six. Recently she was working on an order for one of the traders in Zuni who had supplied silver bands with the stamps already on them (although she knows all the processes involved in working silver). The bracelets were then set with square turquoises; however she will make round sets or use coral for special orders (Fig. 118). Eleanor buys turquoise by the piece, cuts and grinds the stones, and places them with a little wax on the tip of a match for setting. Generally she makes three- or four-row bracelets, sometimes six and once seven. She cuts her own housings from silver and bends them around the stones, then paints solder on the bracelet and finally melts silver drops from a wire to complete the process. In the past she has done the dot-and-dash style and now makes about twenty bracelets a week. Her son and grandson work in their own style of channelwork, flowers, butterflies, and Thunderbirds, and her daughter, next door, does butterflies. The row style used to be popular in the pueblo and she thinks it probably began around 1950 which is about the same time, or a little later, that Clark said he started doing row work.

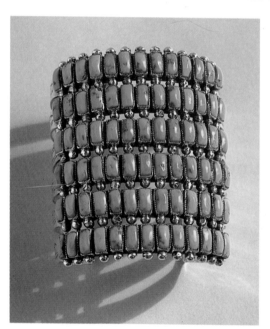

Figure 118. Six-row bracelet by Eleanor Ahiyite

Figure 119. Lorraine Laweka

LORRAINE LAWEKA

Lorraine (Fig.119) learned by watching her mother Elizabeth Cooche do inlay and channelwork jewelry. Her father, Bennie Laweka, did row bracelets and she followed in his style, starting first with clusterwork necklaces and bracelets and then moving to smaller stones in designs called snake eye and dot-and-dash, descriptive of the appearance of the stones. She sets the fine stones and her daughter, Darlene Bobelu, does the silverwork for her, although her son Gomeo Bobelu helps with the larger stonework that involves cutting or slicing the big blocks of turquoise. Lorraine sells in the village and gets orders from Gallup dealers. She used Lone Mountain turquoise in the past, but has switched to Kingman, Sleeping Beauty, and some Chinese stones for the clusterwork. She uses toothpicks to mount the stones but sometimes loses them because they are so small.

Even within a simple style such as row work there are variations such as the number of rows that are joined, whether the stones are round or square, alternating shapes (dot-and-dash), and the size of the stones (snake eyes). The nature of this style means that it is appropriate only for bracelets and rings.

CLUSTERWORK

THIS STYLE CAME TO BE THOUGH OF AS TYPI-CALLY ZUNI EARLY IN THE TWENTIETH CEN-TURY. ALTHOUGH ZUNI SILVERSMITHING AT FIRST RESEMBLED NAVAJO WORK, AFTER THEY LEARNED TO SET STONES, THE ZUNI QUICKLY BEGAN TO MOUNT MANY SETS IN ONE PIECE AS THEIR ANASAZI ANCESTORS BEFORE THEM HAD DONE. THE CLUSTERS RESEMBLE FLOWERS OR PLANT FORMS, SOMEWHAT LIKE THE LARGE FLOWERS ON THE SIDES OF POT-TERY JARS. JEWELRY IN THIS STYLE IS STILL PRIZED BY YOUNG AND OLD ALIKE WITHIN THE PUEBLO AND THE ARTIST WHOSE WORK IS MOST COVETED IS ALICE QUAM.

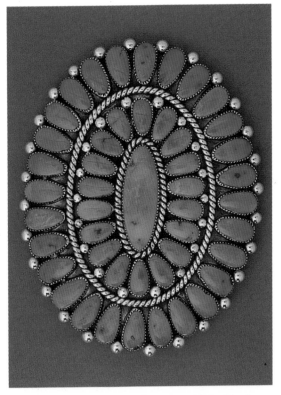

Figure 120. Pin by Alice Quam

ALICE QUAM

Alice is known for using large, well-polished stones and she only buys the best Sleeping Beauty turquoise. It can take her as long as two to three hours to pick enough well-matched stones for one necklace and they are expensive at $75 to $84 per ounce. She will also work in coral, but it is becom-ing difficult to get large pieces. She tried shell but doesn't like it, nor does she like Chinese turquoise, which is much too green for her taste and often has too much matrix. She has been working with her husband Duane since 1945 when he returned from the Second World War, he doing the silver-work and she the stone setting. They both learned from her parents, Wayne and Doris Ondelacy, who were prominent makers of cluster jewelry from the 1930s to the 1950s. (Fig. 123). Buyers come to Alice now and she doesn't have to take her work around to traders or dealers in Gallup

anymore. Alice makes her own housing and blos-soms and used to make her own wire but now uses commercial 26 gauge or 28 gauge for smaller pieces. She keeps sample sets to match for her next pieces of jewelry. Her favorite set is pear-shaped with plain wire about the bezel or housing and a twisted wire border (Fig. 120).

Her daughter Lorraine Waatsa lives next door and does the same type of work but uses a variety of materials, including Chinese turquoise, coral, jet, and lapis (Figs. 120–122). Lorraine is married to Luwayne Waatsa, brother of Bryant Waatsa, Jr. She also won a prize for a cluster pin in gold and opal. Alice used to work in gold herself, but hasn't since 1975. Another daughter, Alvina, lives in Albuquerque and works in the nugget style. Alice's grandchildren started to make jewelry, but didn't have the patience for it—a not uncommon occurrence these days.

Figure 121. Coral bracelet by Lorraine Quam Waatsa

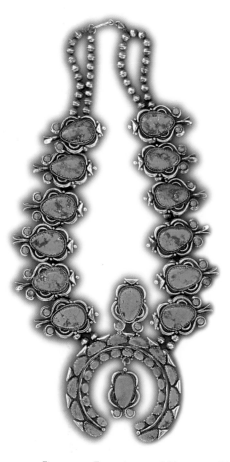

Figure 123. Turquoise squash blossom necklace by Warren and Doris Ondelacy. Private Collection

Figure 122. Turquoise pin by Lorraine Quam Waatsa

PETITPOINT

BONNIE QUAM

Petitpoint and needlepoint are refinements of the cluster style. In petitpoint the stones are small, pointed at one end and rounded at the other. In needlepoint, the tiny stones are pointed at both ends.

Bonnie (Figs. 124–126) was born in 1936 and has been making jewelry since she was eighteen years old. She learned from her husband John Quam. At first she just cut the stones, but then they switched and now she does all the silverwork. Bonnie started with large stones and got progressively smaller and now makes only petitpoint, but in all forms. She sells at Zuni and has won prizes at the Gallup Ceremonial.

Figure 125. Bonnie Quam shaping bezel out of sheet silver

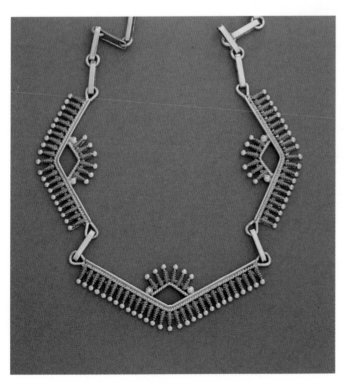

Figure 124. Turquoise petitpoint choker necklace by Bonnie Quam

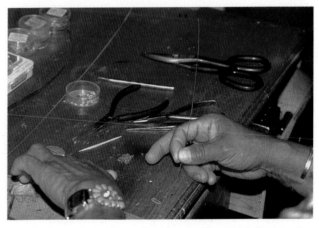

Figure 126. Bonnie Quam's sets and toothpicks for mounting

Figure 127. Turquoise needlepoint necklace
by Bryant Waatsa, Jr.

BRYANT WAATSA, JR.

Bryant learned to make silver by sitting down at a table and watching his father, Bryant Waatsa, at work and believes his father invented the needlepoint technique. This is a natural consequence of the clusterwork aesthetic that encourages the use of increasingly smaller stones. Most workers in needlepoint started with larger stones and found they could create a dazzlingly intricate effect by using increasingly finer sets. In this style, in contrast to that of Alice Quam, the buyer is paying a high price not so much for the carat weight of the stones, as for the incredible labor of cutting and mounting hundreds of minute pieces. C.G. Wallace claims that he encouraged needlepoint during the Depression because it was hard to get good large pieces of turquoise. He collected bags of scraps and asked the jewelers to be creative with small stones. Furthermore, he claims the Dishta family were the first needlepoint workers (Wallace ms.). Bryant started out doing inlay, but he always wanted to do needlepoint like his father. First he prepares his silver backing sheet and then decorates it with stamps and other devices. Next he makes his bezels, first using a gauge to cut the teeth evenly. He specializes in choker necklaces using his own handmade chains with matching earrings. When we interviewed him he had an order for a traditional squash blossom necklace in needlepoint set with Sleeping Beauty turquoise—six blossoms on a side. The silver dangles on the bottom of his pieces are his trademark (Fig. 127). He will work in coral but thinks it is more difficult to use than turquoise. Bryant sells mostly in Zuni and tries to spread his work around among the dealers so there is not too much in one place. He also does repair work for Turquoise Village, a dealer in Zuni.

Figure 128. Edith Tsabetsaye wearing one of her older style necklaces

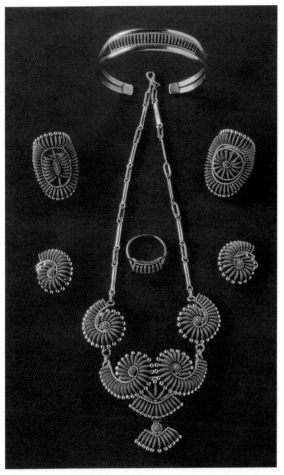

Figure 129. Needlepoint set by Edith Tsabetsaye

EDITH TSABETSAYE

Edith (Fig.128) made her first cluster necklace in 1962 by watching her parents Joe and Susan Tsabetsaye, although she had started in grade school by making crosses and small post earrings. She has six sisters and two brothers, four of whom are artists. She used to make belts, but now does small bracelets, rings, and necklaces in needlepoint and prefers to do special pieces only for the Gallup Ceremonial and the Santa Fe Indian Market.

Refusing to make the same design twice, Edith in fact thinks up a totally new design each year for one special piece. In addition, she has developed a new type of needlepoint that is even more difficult to make, using stones that are raised or curved like crescent moons (Fig. 130). She will make only two or three large necklaces a year, each containing five to six hundred of these sets, and fills orders from collectors and dealers all over the country. Her correspondence with enthusiasts

Figure 130. Raised needlepoint rings by Edith Tsabetsaye

of her work has become extensive and her awards include a First Prize at the Museum of Northern Arizona Zuni show, a Blue Ribbon at the Great Western Show in Pasadena, and a Blue Ribbon at a Tohono O'odham show.

ALONG WITH CLUSTERWORK, MOSAIC IN ALL ITS MANY VARIATIONS IS THE MOST COMMON STYLE AT ZUNI TODAY. ACCORDING TO TRADERS MIKE KIRK AND C.G. WALLACE, IT BEGAN IN THE 1920S AS A RESULT OF THE UNCOVERING OF THE PREHISTORIC MOSAIC JEWELRY AT *HAWIKKU*. THE ANCIENT JEWELRY WAS MADE BY CUTTING SMALL TURQUOISE BITS AND ARRANGING THEM ON A WAX-COVERED WOOD BACKING. THE TECHNIQUE WAS ADAPTED BY CUTTING STONES OF ALL TYPES AND GLUING THEM TO A SILVER BACKING, AND IT REQUIRES A GREAT DEAL OF PRECISION IN STONE CUTTING TO MAKE THE PIECES FIT. FIGURES 131–137 SHOW A RANGE OF EARLY MOSAIC PIECES DATING FROM 1925 TO 1959.

Top: Figure 131. Mosaic bracelet with *Hawikku* pottery design by Dan Simplicio, 1938. The Heard Museum

Figure 132. Eagle Dancer mosaic by Bruce Zunie, 1925 The Heard Museum.

Figure 133. Olla Maiden mosaic by Sam Poblano, 1939. The Heard Museum

There are many variations of mosaic inlay on silver which have developed in the past seventy years. However, there is an intriguing bracelet collected by Matilda Coxe Stevenson prior to her last visit in 1902 and now in the National Museum of Natural History in Washington (Fig. 138). The bracelet made by Kuwishte (Kuwichte), the late-nineteenth-century blacksmith at the village (Adair 1944, 122), has three turquoise stones set not in the usual manner by making a housing or bezel around each stone and soldering it on to a silver backing, but by cutting a hole into the silver and quite literally inlaying each set into the bracelet. A further variation of mosaic style is channelwork (Figs. 139–144), the use of soldered silver compartments. The stones are cut to fit into the silverwork, creating repetitive geometric patterns. The style has been in existence since 1940 or perhaps a little earlier.

Figure 134. Turquoise mosaic butterfly belt by Lambert Homer, 1946. The Heard Museum

Figure 135. Mosaic Sword Swallower by Bruce Zunie. The Heard Museum

Figure 136. Mosaic Koshare by Lambert Homer, 1949. The Heard Museum

Figure 137. Mosaic Fire God by Walter Nahktewa, 1959. The Heard Museum

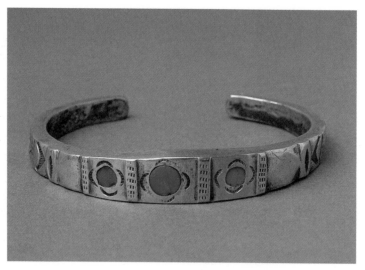

Figure 138. Silver bracelet with turquoise inlay made by Kuwishte. The National Museum of Natural History

Figure 139. Turquoise channelwork turtle by Juan Dedios. The Heard Museum

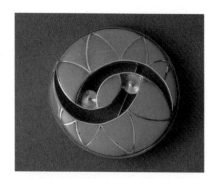

Figure 140. Turquoise channel "hummingbird" design pin by Varden Vacit

Figure 141. Coral channelwork bracelet by Rickell and Glendora Booqua

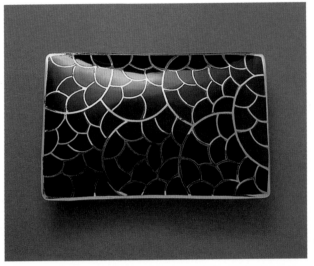

Figure 142. Jet channelwork belt buckle in fishscale pattern by Carmichael Haloo

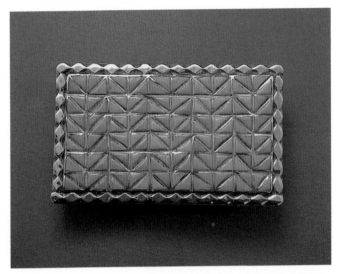

Figure 143. Turquoise channelwork belt buckle by Jack Bobelu

Figure 144. Channelwork bracelet by Eldred Seotewa

Figure 145. Linda Hustito Wheeler at workbench

Figure 146. Knifewing mosaic by Alonzo Hustito

LINDA HUSTITO WHEELER

Linda (Fig. 145) learned to make clusterwork jewelry from her mother-in-law and later did the same type of work with her father, Alonzo Hustito. Alonzo was the originator of the Rainbow Man and Knifewing figures in jewelry and it wasn't until he died in 1989 or 1990 that she took over his work and taught herself the mosaic style.

Knifewing is a mythological being with wings covered in flint blades who sweeps down from the sky and carries off beautiful Zuni girls. The Rainbow Man is associated with summer rains and the beautiful colors of the heavens. Neither of these figures are kachinas and, although important in Zuni traditions, do not have the same power as the kachinas. This may explain why jewelers used these beings in their work at first before venturing on to the more powerful and potentially controversial beings. Linda keeps a sample of her father's work (Fig. 146) and continues in his style. The silver decoration is the same in each inlay piece, but the combinations of colored stones are usually different. Her mother and father collaborated on their work, but Linda does both the silverwork and stone cutting. Not only does she keep a piece by her father as a model, but she has a board he used to work with, with patterns and sizes cut in.

Linda has done channelwork, inlay, and cluster, and works on as many as twenty pieces at one time in various techniques. Behind her home is a modern shed in which she uses her motor and grinding wheel. She does other work in her kitchen. To attach the stones to the silver she uses a modern glue called Hot Stuff instead of the older Duco cement.

Linda Hustito Wheeler passed away in the summer of 1994.

Figure 147. Knifewing mosaic
by Linda Hustito Wheeler

Figure 148. Rainbow Man
by Linda Hustito Wheeler

Figure 149. Linda Hustito Wheeler selecting stone

Figure 150. Ed Beyuka

ED BEYUKA

Ed Beyuka (Fig.150) uses a variation on the mosaic technique with some silver compartments supporting sections of his mosaic work. Since he generally makes large, complex kachina figures (Figs.151–154) as bolo ties or a combination bolo and standing figure for tabletop display, the silver divides sections of the piece and gives it visual definition as well as structural support.

Ed served in World War II and was captured in the Philippines by the Japanese Army and taken on the Bataan Death March. After the war, Ed received a disability discharge. During the 1950s he was a guard at Fort Wingate, a weapons storage facility forty miles north of Zuni, and then decided to take his high school equivalency examination in order to enter St. Joseph's College in Albuquerque. He left college after a semester and returned to Zuni. Although he had watched his parents making jewelry while he was growing up, he didn't make any himself until 1956. He practiced in the evenings while his family was at the Night Dances. Then he taught his wife Madeline to work with him—she did the inlay

Figure 151. Eagle Dancer by Ed Beyuka

and he did the silverwork. Her fingers were very deft and she did finer work than he, but after they divorced he learned to do the inlay as well as the silver. The silver backing is cut freehand, then Ed attaches the housings with solder during the day and cuts the stones in the evening. Ed even makes the silver baskets some of the kachinas carry (to put bad children in) out of interlaced wire and hand-fashions the drums which are the tips of the bolos (Fig. 152). His oldest son, Jonathan, does finer work than his father; another son, Filbert, specializes in Buffalo Dancers and Plains Indians. A daughter, Christine, makes small jewelry with single stones. It is not considered proper for a woman to make kachina jewelry, although a few Zuni women have done so. Ed sells mainly in other parts of the country, not in Zuni, and hopes to become a retailer traveling around the country doing shows. He cannot work just at any time, he has to have inspiration. "I want to make my work the best I can because it may be the last I make."

Figure 152. *A:doshle* by Ed Beyuka

Figure 153. Female *A:doshle* by Ed Beyuka

Figure 154. Fire God by Ed Beyuka

Figure 155. Andrew Dewa

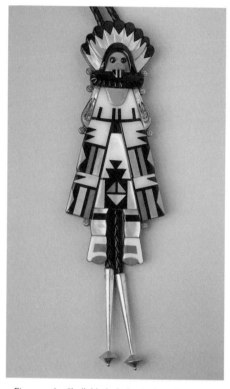

Figure 156. Sha'lak'o bolo by Andrew Dewa, 1976.
The Heard Museum

ANDREW AND DON DEWA

Brothers Andrew and Don Dewa work in a variety or substyle of mosaic work called Sun Face. That is, the central or most important motif is the mask of the sun, which is a stylized human face with rectangular eyes and mouth surrounded by a full circle of eagle feathers. The usual colors of the face are turquoise on the left, coral on the right, and white or yellow on the chin. Making the Sun Face does honor to the Sun Father.

Andrew, the elder brother (Fig. 155), learned from their parents Leroy and Anita Dewa by making small pieces in cluster and nugget style when he was seventeen. Occasionally he still produces a clusterwork piece and has also made Rainbow Men and Knifewings. He now does a distinctive type of mosaic inlay which is three-

Figure 157. Sun Face choker by Andrew Dewa

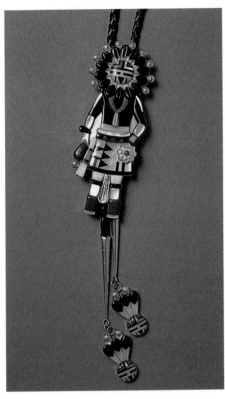

Figure 158. Sun bolo by Andrew Dewa

Figure 159. Don Dewa

dimensional, raised, and now also carved (Fig. 157). Andrew has won many prizes, probably, he thinks, because of the perfection and smoothness of his settings. Most of his customers are from outside the pueblo. Not only are Andrew's stones cut well, but the colors are well matched. His eagle feathers are the traditional color—white shell with jet tips. It was Andrew who invented the variation of the Sun Face with only two feathers.

Don (Fig. 159) didn't start making small cluster-work chokers, rings, and earrings until he got out of the service in 1970. Five or six years ago he learned mosaic inlay from his wife Velma's mother, Loretta Quam Eriacho, sister of Ellen Quam Quandelacy. Although Velma is a jeweler, she has her own style—channelwork—and they don't work together. Like his older brother, Don

Figure 160. Belt buckle by Don Dewa

Figure 161. Don Dewa finishing a spinner bracelet

Figure 162. Spinner bracelet by Don Dewa

makes Sun Face mosaics in bracelets, rings, and bolos. His specialty is what he calls a spinner bracelet: the Sun Face is mounted on a silver wire which allows it to spin to a second, more simply designed face (Fig. 162). He can make one or two of these elaborate bracelets in a week. Most of his sales are to traders within the village. Don worked about six years for the Bureau of Indian Affairs, but quit in the early 1980s when he found he could make more money from jewelry.

GUS PANTEAH

Gus was born in 1939 and learned silversmithing from his mother when he was about twelve. She taught him and his sister, Rena King, clusterwork during the summer, when school was out. In 1965 Gus and his sister were the first to work in the modern or abstract style of mosaic inlay. This newer style has become popular with many younger artists and indeed can be found in the jewelry of Navajo and Hopi artists as well. Many members of Gus's family work in the new style, especially his nephews Duran and Arnie Gasper, whom he taught to do mosaic work, and also his younger brother Martin (Fig. 163) and his sons Malcolm and Craig.

Continuing the old practice of one artist making mosaic stone sets and another setting them in silver, Gus orders Apache *Gan* Dancer sets from Martin and sets them in his own silver mounts. The *Gan* Dancer was first used in jewelry by Gus's cousin Lambert Homer. He does special orders for local traders and sets up shows of his work. Since he is now a tribal councilman, Gus doesn't have much time for his jewelry, although he likes to try unusual things. He was the first person back in 1955 to do silver drops around diamond-shaped sets. He has also tried inlay on glass for the 1993 Indian Market in Santa Fe and a small altar which opened up to reveal a bear fetish.

Figure 163. Bracelet and necklace set by Martin and Esther Panteah

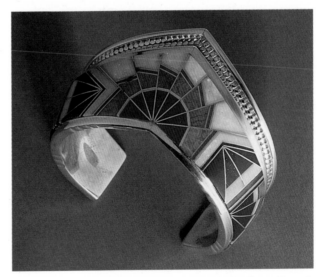

Figure 164. Opal mosaic bracelet by Clayton Panteah

Figure 165. Duran Gasper at silver working table

ARNIE AND DURAN GASPER

The two brothers live near one another in the modern housing of Blackrock. Duran is twenty-six and learned clusterwork from his mother, Rose Gasper, in 1987, but learned inlay from his brother Arnie. Both brothers worked in the Gallup workshop of Navajo jeweler Ray Tracey. Ray designed the jewelry and had the silver machine-cast, but Duran and Arnie designed the inlay. After working for a year in Gallup, Duran decided to work on his own at home. Duran had turned an old school bus into a workshop but, when he moved to Blackrock, there was no place to park it so he turned one of his closets into a studio for the stone cutting (Fig. 29). The silver work and finishing is done under a window in one of the bedrooms (Fig. 165). A constant stream of water plays over his cutting wheel to take up the dust and keep the stone from breaking. Duran uses all natural stones, both traditional and more modern ones such as lapis and opal. Silver strips are incorporated for decorative effect, but not soldered in, being treated as all the other stones. When the stones are all cut perfectly, Duran knocks out the sets, does a final finishing of the stones, textures the silver base, and then sets them in with epoxy glue. He also coats the top surface with epoxy to protect the stones.

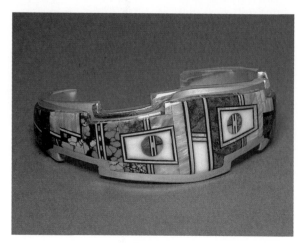

Figure 166. Bracelet by Duran Gasper

Although Duran's aunt, Rena Panteah King, showed him how to solder in the sixth and seventh grades, he didn't really pick up on it until recently. At first Duran used his brother Arnie's equipment, but bought his own with money he had saved from the service. Generally he spends a week or two preparing the silverwork for a number of pieces and then moves into the other room and cuts the stones all at one time. Inspiration for the jagged abstract designs on the pendants and bracelets for which he is famous came from a rock formation in the Twin Buttes area of the reservation (Fig. 166).

Arnie (Fig. 167) started making small stud earrings in the eighth grade and later learned inlaying from his uncle Gus Panteah. After he graduated from high school in 1989 he worked in Gallup, first as a silver caster and then for four years for Navajo jeweler Ray Tracey. He learned a lot about mosaic inlay from Ray and gained experience on the road selling their work. Arnie has won prizes for his work at the annual Zuni show at the Museum of Northern Arizona (Fig. 168). The lightning bracelet was his idea, although Duran's is similar but more tapered at the ends. When the killer in the Academy Award-winning movie *Silence of the Lambs* was shown wearing his triangular pendant, he got a rush of orders (Fig.169). By and large he sells to dealers within the village and had a commission to make a channelwork crown for Miss Indian New Mexico. Arnie is interested in other art forms and makes an occasional fetish. When he was in high school he won an award for his pottery. Arnie is married to DeeDee, sister of Olivia Panteah, and she in turn has picked up inlay work, mostly small rings and bracelets, in the last three years by watching him.

Figure 167. Arnie and DeeDee Gasper

Figure 169. Pendant by Arnie Gasper

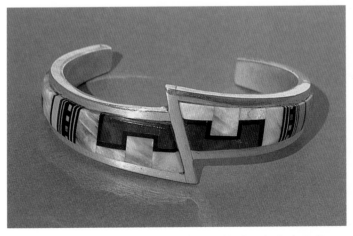

Figure 168. Bracelet by Arnie Gasper

Figure 170. Olivia Panteah
Top Right: Figure 171. Bolo by Olivia Panteah

Figure 172. Bracelet by Olivia Panteah

Figure 173. Mudhead bolo by Rosalie Pinto

OLIVIA PANTEAH

Olivia's (Fig. 170) whole family made jewelry and she learned from her grandfather Bert Quam, brother of Annie Gasper and Ellen Quandelacy. As a girl she remembers watching her grandfather work with an old-fashioned pump or bow drill and hand grinder in the late 1960s. When he wasn't around she would practice on his tools with scraps of glass. Bert passed on in 1976. After she married Ronnie Calavaza they made kachina style mosaic inlay together, but when they divorced in 1986 she moved to Florida. Ronnie and his mother, Rosalie Pinto, specialize in a raised inlay—stones set on other stones in kachina patterns, especially Mudhead Clowns (Fig. 173). While living in Florida Olivia continued to make jewelry and did shows at various galleries. Because of her mother's health she returned to Zuni to live with her.

Now Olivia no longer makes kachina jewelry, but whatever abstract design comes to mind. Each design is different with no repetition and no use of patterns. Although she can make all forms, Olivia prefers to make choker necklace and bracelet sets. Olivia describes her style as three-level or three-dimensional inlay (also called raised inlay by others) (Figs. 171 and 172). In the past she has experimented with nontraditional stones such as lapis and sugilite, but now prefers the older Zuni stones and strong color contrasts. Olivia feels very strongly that her jewelry is part of her self. She won't sell to buyers who don't appreciate her work.

Olivia's children, Shannon, aged thirteen, and Rodney, eighteen, help her out. Rodney is especially helpful with the stone cutting as the silverwork takes most of her time. This is a reversal of the usual Zuni practice of a man in the family doing the silver and the woman stone cutting and setting. Because she works in a bedroom she wants to get a blower to vent the dust from the stonework.

Figure 174. Veronica Poblano

VERONICA POBLANO

Veronica (Fig.174) is the daughter of stone cutter and jeweler Leo Poblano, who died thirty-two years ago when Veronica was ten. She learned mainly by asking her father questions. He worked with very large stones, using a wide wheel with a bucket at the bottom to collect water that he dripped over the wheel. Her mother continued making kachina style jewelry after his death. Both of her parents did kachina inlay which was set by Navajo silversmiths. Veronica believes that many pieces in museum collections that are credited to Leekya Deyuse are really the work of her father. His work usually includes small dots of colored inlay.

Daisy Hooee Nampeyo, granddaughter of the famous Hopi potter Nampeyo, married Leo Poblano in 1939. As a young woman, Daisy studied art in Paris at L'ecole des Beaux Arts. When she moved to Zuni, Leo taught her silversmithing and mosaic inlay. She started to experiment with new designs, the first of which was a Hopi maiden in mosaic set on a silver box. Her training as a sculptor led her to add three-dimensional and carved details to the inlay as well as making small

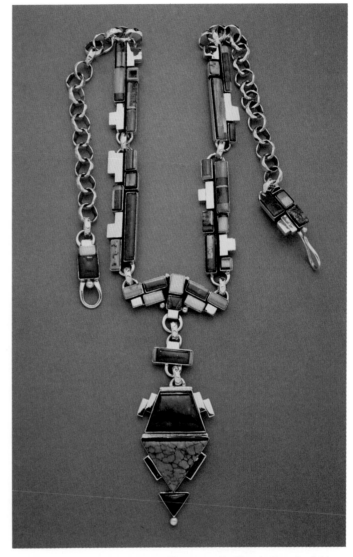

Figure 175. Necklace by Veronica Poblano

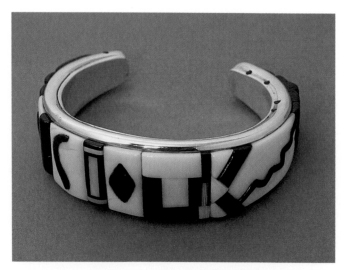

Figure 176. Bracelet by Veronica Poblano

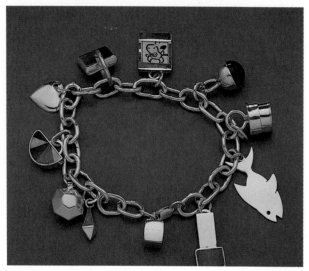

Figure 177. Charm bracelet
by Dylan Poblano

carvings out of turquoise nuggets. Leo also began experimenting with new designs and the couple sold all of their work to C.G. Wallace (Fowler 1977, 50–59).

Veronica began doing mosaic work for Gallup dealer Joe Tanner when she was fourteen or fifteen. Veronica is proud of the fact that she never makes the same design twice (Figs. 175 and 176) and copyrights each piece and sends the paperwork to Washington. Her work is sold mainly outside of Zuni and she has had a show at the Eiteljorg Museum in Indianapolis and one in Tokyo. She recently won the Myerson Award for her booth at Indian Market. Her seventeen-year-old son Dylan started working at age eight and in 1993 won an award at the Zuni Show at the Museum of Northern Arizona for a clever charm bracelet (Fig. 177). Her daughter does fine beadwork and another son, Brad, does multicolor inlay in the contemporary style. Other than her parents' influence she feels her experience as a beautician and the training she received in color charting has been the most help in her work. She constantly experiments with new stones.

Figure 178. Long Hair kachina
by Leo Poblano, 1945. The Heard Museum

Figure 179 Antelope bowguard
by Leo Poblano, 1948. The Heard Museum

Figure 181. Duck-in-flight pin
by Leo Poblano, 1951. The Heard Museum

Figure 180. Shell with inlaid Fire God by Leo Poblano.
The National Museum of the American Indian

ALTHOUGH THIS DESCRIPTION SOUNDS LIKE DOUBLETALK, IT IS AN ACCURATE TERM FOR THIS TECHNIQUE WHICH HAS BEEN IN USE SINCE THE 1970S. IN SOME WAYS IT IS SIMILAR TO HOPI OVERLAY WORK. THE JEWELER PREPARES A SIMPLE BACKING OF SILVER, THEN PREPARES A SECOND PIECE OF THE SAME SIZE AND SHAPE AND THE DESIGN IS CUT OUT WITH A SAW. THE CUTOUT IS SOLDERED ONTO THE PLAIN PIECE. IN HOPI WORK THE DESIGN IN THE CUTOUT AREA IS ENHANCED BY TEXTURING WITH A TOOL OR TARNISHING WITH A CHEMICAL; THE ZUNI ARTIST INLAYS THE DETAILS OF THE DESIGN WITH MULTICOLORED STONES.

Figure 182. Koshare belt by Myron Edaakie

Figure 183. Myron Edaakie sawing silver overlay

Figure 184. Hummingbird bolo by Dennis Edaakie

DENNIS EDAAKIE

Dennis's father, Merle Edaakie, was a contemporary of Teddy Weahkee. He made the stonework for Knifewing and Rainbow Man figures for C.G. Wallace and the Vanderwagens, which they had set by Navajo silversmiths. Dennis had not made any jewelry before he was drafted into the army in 1950. After his return from Korea, Dennis worked at a truck stop and began to sell some of the work of his uncle, Jacob Haloo. It was very popular, so he decided to watch his uncle and learn how to make his style. Although some said he copied his uncle's work, Dennis feels his pieces are much more detailed.

Gallup traders Leon and Ruth Ingram asked him to make something special for the Gallup Ceremonial in 1970. They looked through a book together and decided on a cardinal pin that captured a First Place ribbon. The Ingrams also asked him to design a pendant that would be reversible without taking it off, so Dennis was the first to devise a pendant on a swivel—hummingbird which reversed to an apple blossom. Even though he has won prizes at the Gallup Ceremonial he doesn't like to show there anymore since his work gets copied. However he participates in shows in Taos and Scottsdale. Nancy Edaakie, his wife, began with leaves and flowers and now does his inlay work. His sons, Myron, Sanford, and Derrick, all make silver in the overlay inlay style (Fig. 183). In addition to birds he likes to inlay bears, wolves, fish, deer, elk, dogs, and he once did a special order of chimpanzees. It takes a great deal of time to design and cut out the inlay for each new design, but then each successive one is easier. The Edaakies were the first family to do the Koshare or Rio Grande Clown design in silver (Fig. 182).

Figure 185. Rolanda Haloo

Left: **Figure 186.** Hummingbird pin by Rolanda Haloo

ROLANDA HALOO

Rolanda (Figs. 185 and 189) is one of the daughters of Jake Haloo, but learned by watching her sisters, Dolly Banteah, Nancy Laconsello, and Lolita Natachu. She tried using bits of worthless sandstone on her sisters' wheels before she tried more expensive materials. She has won many ribbons, including Best of Show in lapidary in Gallup and the Heard Museum. The Knifewing and Rainbow figures she uses were her father's (Figs. 35, 187, and 188). She casts her own rings, and pin and bolo backings. Rolanda's work is more naturalistic—bear, deer, and birds—while that of her sisters is more geometric. She prefers mostly Zuni designs, rather than the animals shown on the wall of her studio. These traditional designs are of course

the Rainbow God and Knifewing, but also butterflies and dragonflies. Rolanda stays away from jet and shell and uses stones such as opals, garnets, and lapis. When she was at St. John's Indian School in Scottsdale she took a jewelry class, and progressed rapidly since she had more experience than the other students. Her eleven-year-old son Colin is already making pendants, and Rolanda was only fourteen when she began. Rolanda uses old cutter blades as templates for her designs, cutting them with a coping saw, and adding details with a dremel drill.

Figure 187. Knifewing bracelet by Rolanda Haloo

Figure 188. Knifewing ring by Rolanda Haloo

Figure 189. Rolando Haloo cutting a stone on diamond wheel

Figure 190. Carlton, Julie, and Alex Jamon

CARLTON JAMON

Carlton (Fig. 190) is one of the founding
members of the Zuni Cultural Arts Council
which promotes local artists and teaches them to
sell directly to the public. He has had shows at the
Ray Tracey Gallery in Santa Fe, Bien Mur in
Albuquerque, and booths at the Santa Fe Indian
Market. Thirty-one-year-old Carlton learned by
watching his grandmother Cornelia Jamon in the
1970s, who in turn learned from her mother,
Winnie Jamon, silversmith for C.G. Wallace.
Carlton won a Blue Ribbon for a gold necklace at
the 1993 Zuni Show at the Museum of Northern
Arizona (Fig. 192). He has been experimenting
with beads such as the ones in this necklace,
employing new materials such as lapis, special
connecting chains, and metal tube beads which he
textures by using a dremel or graver. Working
with gold is a bit different from silver—it is
springier, taking four hammer blows to fashion it
to one for silver. Carlton does not make kachina
jewelry, but has become well known for his fetish-
style hollow silver bear which he has been making
since 1985 (Fig. 193). Now his wife Julie and
sometimes his young son, Alex (Fig. 194), help
him. Julie works on the cutting, stringing, and
polishing while he solders, inlays, and sets the
stones.

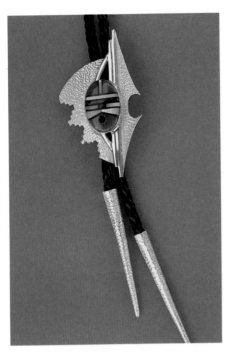

Figure 191. Bolo by Carlton Jamon

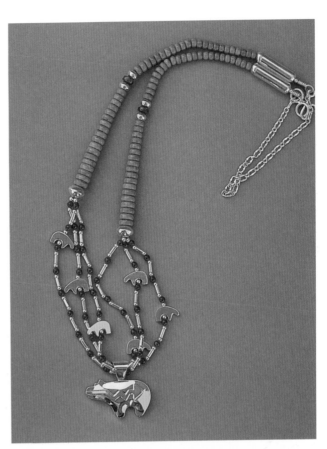

Figure 193. Bear necklace by Carlton Jamon

Figure 192. Gold necklace of handmade beads
and Butterfly Maiden. Carlton Jamon

Figure 194. Julie and Alex Jamon stringing beads

Figure 195. Smokey Gchachu

SMOKEY GCHACHU

Smokey (Fig. 195) learned by watching and helping his mother, Ruby, and has been working on his own since 1975 or 1976. He also works in construction. These skills have allowed him to add an addition to his home and studio. He also bought books on Southwestern jewelry to learn new techniques. He makes inlay and needlepoint and a combination of these two techniques and plans to do inlay with diamonds. His needlepoint has won prizes and he has devised a type of reversible needlepoint that is turquoise on one side and coral on the other. He has had a booth at Indian Market but feels his work is too expensive and sells better in galleries. Going on from reversible needlepoint, Smokey is experimenting with new and unusual styles (Figs. 196 and 197). His work with diamonds and hanging branches of coral submitted to the 1993 Zuni Show at the Museum Northern Arizona puzzled the judges because it "didn't look Zuni."

Figure 196. Necklace by Smokey Gchachu

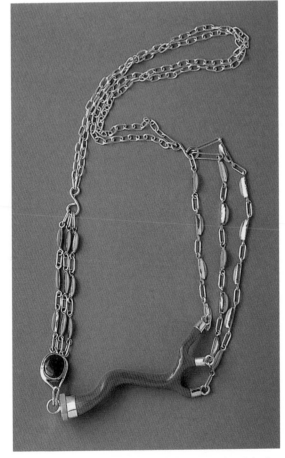

Figure 197. Necklace by Smokey Gchachu

PART IV

A Conversation between
Charles Hustito and
Jim Ostler

CHARLES HUSTITO IS THE SON OF ALONZO AND HELEN HUSTITO. HE IS MARRIED TO ROSE HUSTITO. TWO SISTERS, LINDA HUSTITO WHEELER AND ERMA HUSTITO, ARE ALSO WELL-KNOWN SILVERSMITHS. HE WAS A MEMBER OF THE ZUNI TRIBAL COUNCIL FROM 1982 TO 1986. IN ADDITION TO BEING A SILVERSMITH HE IS A KEEN STUDENT OF THE HISTORY OF ZUNI AND OF ZUNI SILVERSMITHING.

Figure 198. Charles Hustito and Jim Ostler

JIM: I have always noted since I first met you (Fig. 198) that you wear a lot of jewelry and you seem very careful about what you wear and I remember at one time there was a hat that you wore and there were a whole lot of pins on it. And that was always interesting to me. I have always been interested in how you select things.

CHARLES: I have always taken it as a mark of prestige. Back in the early days, when I was growing up, I used to notice the Vanderwagen traders—especially this one man I used to know. He ran the café. His name was Ed Vanderwagen. He used to wear this one piece of jewelry all the time and it distinguished him from all the rest of the people I knew here. So, I became very good friends with him. I don't know what he saw in me, but he always used to tell me how to carry on our jewelry making business and learn the trade from my father and to maintain that (Figs. 199 and 200).

He said that in the long run, in the years to come, it would give you a livelihood or—if you go into higher education—it will be something that you will always know how to do. It could be a

secondary trade or a primary trade, however you want to work it. You could work as a full-time jewelry artist and you could use your education in a consultant type of business.

So I always kept that in mind. Round about when I was eleven years old I moved down into Arizona to live with Grandfather who was working for the Southern Pacific Railroad. What a difference! I guess you would say a cultural shock. I didn't see anybody wearing any jewelry except ties and little tie pins that you buy from the jewelry stores where you buy your diamonds and stuff like that. I adapted to that kind of culture too, and I felt real respectable.

My grandfather worked for the Southern Pacific Railroad, but he didn't forget his language but he was kind of tongue-tied when he wanted to talk in Zuni. When we moved down there, he always used to tell us, "Talk in English." And I said, "But let me talk in Zuni." I wanted to use my language, because before he had nobody to talk to in Zuni. He was tongue-tied—he couldn't pronounce some of the words right. He used to be funny—we used

Figure 199. Alonzo Hustito

to teach him how to say this and that. But his knowledge of Zuni language was in his head. It's just that to verbalize it was kind of difficult for him after not talking to anybody for so long. I guess that happens even now. The English language has become our primary language, with our kids, too.

There's so much change in our lifestyle that I guess we want everything to happen quickly now. Like, for instance, we don't have the storytellers now. In my days they used to have storytellers that would tell us stories. That was our entertainment. We were fortunate we had a radio, but that was it. But our lifestyle has tremendously changed with the coming of electricity. First it was radios, phonographs. Of course I grew up with television down in the Valley of the Sun, but here it was strange. It was something very new. The first television I saw in Gallup when I came back one summer was at Castings Furniture. And it was the blurriest thing that you can see, but people stood around the window squinting their eyes to see what the heck was showing. Then, after that they started having television, telephones, and what not, what we have now.

JIM: How long were you down in Arizona?

CHARLES: I guess from the fifth grade on up to when I started having some difficulty with Grandfather around about when I was in my sophomore year. I guess it was right after they built the high school that I came back. I came back, but I didn't want to go here. I went to St. Anthony School, so when I came they were busing the students into the Cathedral High School [in Gallup]. In my sophomore year I was going to Cathedral High School, then the following year they couldn't afford to transport the kids so I had to enroll here—I had nobody to take me back and forth. I had some problems with the school here. Academically it was, you know, not really there. In my junior year they were teaching me something that I had already had at eighth grade level. I got accused of cheating—I got

Figure 200. Charles Hustito holding a bowguard by his father

Figure 201. Rainbow Man pin by Alonzo Hustito

Figure 202. Finished Rainbow Man in Alonzo Hustito's workshop

kinds of designs because from a distance you can see and you can distinguish the colors, and the different textures of the stones that are set in it (Fig. 202). It stands out from a distance better than something with very small intricate pieces—you don't know what the heck it is until you come up to it very close and almost stare at an individual.

My father worked on that kind of patterns or designs. My mother would put the pieces together and my father would do the housing for the inlay. Then, when they finished it, my mother or father would shape it. For the Knifewing there would be the headdress (it would be a pyramid shape), the head (would be oval), the wings, the body, the dress (as a kilt), then the legs. They would shape it out with those individual pieces and then my father would make the housings out of bezel.

In those days everything was done from scratch. You would buy a housing plate and then put the teeth in it. Then you would cut the strips and make your housing. Now you buy everything premanufactured. My parents would reuse any scraps of silver they had left over to make small drops of silver as decoration around the housings. In those days whatever was left over was used—you would even gather the filings. Those were remelted and used for other things, such as an ornament around the design. Very seldom did my father take silver scraps back to the trader and sell them for a sheet of silver.

accused of being a smart guy. I kind of got remarks from the teachers. I couldn't handle it so I dropped out. Dropped out of high school.

When I came back to Zuni and my parents had always worked on inlay jewelry. People sometimes confuse the terms. Channel inlay work is where you make a silver piece and then you do all the intricate silver—the outlining—and then the inner parts according to how you want to design it. That's basically what you call channel inlay work. The way that my parents used to work was to put all the different stones together, grind them, shape them and then glue them [mosaic inlay]. They made Knifewings and Thunderbirds—well that's what they called it. Right now it kind of got into a modern version where they started putting on the wings and they started calling it Thunderbird, but back in those days the traders called it the Knifewing bird (Fig.146).

It was kind of a crude, simple design—not too intricate in detail. My father worked in those

When I was growing up we didn't have electricity and it was all done with a hand grinding wheel—the buffing and the grinding of all the stones and everything else. In those days there were no electric drills or cutters like we have now. They basically used a sidecutter to cut the stone and to grind it down to shape. My parents would look for thin pieces of turquoise so that they didn't waste too much of it by using a sidecutter in trying to flatten it out. The shell and other kinds of stones that they used normally came flat. They used abalone shell instead of coral for the red part of it, and sometimes on a special order they would use the back side of an abalone shell where it has many colors.

JIM: Could you tell us a little more about the tools. What sort of grinders are we talking about, big ones, little ones?

CHARLES: The hand grinder has basically a wheel that we use today. I think it is the kind of grinding tool that was used in the blacksmith shop for fine smoothing out when they do welding. I always remember that it had one attachment where you attached a dresser, a wheel dresser. It is all made out of steel and you used that to even out the wheel, 'cause eventually, when you use it daily, it begins to make impressions on the wheel and when you are trying to do an inlay work you are really trying to really avoid any gaps in between. That's why you have to use the dresser to dress out the wheel so that you get that fine cut of straight line.

My mother used to use two kinds. One of them, a medium or coarse wheel, was for fast cutting. The fine was used after you get through with shaping to do the surface so that it will come out real smooth. In those days I don't believe that there was any such thing as Bright Boy polishing compound so that real fine grinding wheel was the one that really did the work. And they had this sandpaper—real fine. I used to get a piece of that and, before they mounted the stones onto the silver, used it until I got a halfway shine on the stones. That cuts a little bit of polishing time. Then they would put the cloth wheel on there and they would use a buffing compound to buff it and then the chamois wheel to bring out the final shine on the silver and the stones. That's basically how our parents worked.

For bolos they would put a little loop in the back to hold the strap. The bolo I'm wearing used to have a strap, until he redid the silver and put a bolo-back on it. In the old days, if you made bolos and stuff like that you would buy the strap and make your own tips, but now they just make the bolos and the dealers and traders have got their own premanufactured tips and straps. Basically, that's how our parents used to work. We didn't have any electricity and there was no television to see, and our parents restricted us from listening to radios, battery operated radios. They didn't have these long-range radio stations. I remember when Del Rio, Texas, was the station we used to catch at nights, and we would listen to it for a while and we would go to bed while they stayed up and worked until I don't know when. They used Coleman lanterns seated right next to the work table to get some light. Of course, in those days, their eyes were still good so they can see better so they can work. Now everybody has got electrical lights, but that's how our parents used to work.

JIM: You described how your father would do the silver work and make the bezels and your mother would do the stone work. You said that all the stones were shaped and fitted together as one piece, and a bezel was made for the whole design.

CHARLES: My mother would put all the details and shaping of the stones. My mother and father would alternate their work. If my father was out doing something else—maybe going after fire-wood or going to the sheep camp or just helping out with his kiva work—then my mother would go ahead and do whatever she had to do.

After they finished shaping the stone and the shell inlay, then they would individually shape the bezel for each element. The headdress, wings, body, kilt, and legs are all mosaics that are shaped individually. When they are done, they soldered housings for each piece and then connected the housings by solder. After that they would cut out a piece of silver and measure just how big the silver plate is going to be to mount the whole design. After soldering the housing onto the plate he would put whatever ornaments he wanted—drops, or other silver dressing that he used—then he would solder those on.

After that is all completed then he would take his coping saw, cut it out, then take a fine file and file out those little nudges and everything like that. After that's done, if they're making pins, he would put the pin, the pin catcher, and the pin holder on the back. After he puts all those things on there, while it's still hot, he dumps it in the acid.

Before acid was used, there was a mine of some minerals—can't remember what they called it—my grandpa used to mine that from somewhere around the Pia Mesa area (see p. 77) They boiled that and dumped in their fine finished silver work. That would remove all the tarnish from the heat—it was a silver cleaner. Take it out, take a steel brush, scrub off all that white thing that forms all around, then you've got clean silver there. After that they would start inlaying the mosaic sets for the headdress, head, body, wings, kilt, and legs. He had a little tool to squeeze the teeth on the housing to hold it in. Then comes the polishing part.

JIM: No glue? So it was mechanical hold—the sets had to fit very closely so that all the pieces would fit together.

CHARLES: There was really no glue. I guess they were real conservative with their materials and they did not want to do too much grinding. When my dad made the housing for it, the setting was high enough to where it was going to fit right into it and the teeth would hold it. There was no backing for it. In those days the glue was hard to come by and they had to make it fit so that the teeth alone would hold the piece together.

JIM: You mentioned your grandfather, was he a silversmith?

CHARLES: No. He was a livestock producer. He was into herding sheep—for other people, too—right off the reservation. Of course, he does his planting of corn, and would go after wood, and that kept him busy.

JIM: Do you know how your father learned silversmithing?

CHARLES: I really don't know how he picked it up. I just remember him doing it, and I guess I

was not that inquisitive to ask how he learned and I always thought that it was a natural thing that I would learn sooner or later. But come to find out later on that you really have to train and to have patience to do that kind of work.

JIM: One of the things that I notice about Zuni jewelry is how tightly things fit. And you helped me understand that when you put a mosaic pattern together the pieces have to fit or they will fall out. But, why are there so many pieces in Zuni jewelry?

CHARLES: We use basically the same colors, but some people like to have a little bit of eccentric kind of pattern or design to distinguish that family's trade. Almost like you see a certain piece of work and you can identify the origins of where that pattern came from even though it is the great-grandchildren who are doing it. But basically it is carried on from generation to generation. I got married into a family that does channelwork and I got into that and I am not carrying on my parents' type of work. But, my sister [Linda] used to do my parents' kind of work. And I thought, "Well, let her carry it on." And I have thought about starting that, but I have to get all those tools together, and that's quite an investment now. But, it's not that I can't do it, but time is of the essence (Fig. 203).

JIM: You said that your mother and father used basic colors. What are those basic colors? And you also said that perhaps to distinguish one family's jewelry from another's that they would use their own selection of colors?

CHARLES: Selection of colors has not that much to do with identity—it is the pattern and design and the nature of silverwork that distinguishes families. We all use coral, turquoise, jet, white shell, pink shell, and abalone shell. I think those are the basic colors we used in the old days. Then, as the jewelry industry started picking up, I think in the 1970s, any kind of stone that could bring a polish, a glitter, they started using it in jewelry. Some of our people adapted to that. I don't think

Figure 203. Linda Hustito Wheeler

it was just a matter of choice, but it was a matter of demand, what the public wanted. And they could easily purchase the raw materials right there in the market.

JIM: But your father and your mother stayed more or less with those six colors.

CHARLES: Basically, yes, they stayed with those colors.

JIM: In Zuni jewelry there's all these colors that are put together in some kind of pattern. In other kinds of jewelry it might not be so colorful. In Navajo jewelry, for example, you don't see that kind of color. You see turquoise stones that are then fixed in place with a bezel and it has a simpler look to it. But Zuni jewelry is very clean and precise and colorful. Why?

CHARLES: My curiosity about that grew as I grew older, and I came back home and started studying

history and different lifestyles of tribes. This all has to do with the Indian traders. The Indian traders here really got the Zuni people into the fine arts because of the Zunis' abilities and artistic skills. Maybe patience was another factor. In our livelihood, talking now on our religious aspect of life, there is a lot of patience that has to go into these rituals and ceremonies, and self-discipline. I think these are the major factors in making the traders realize that there are these people that have these types of abilities.

Zuni jewelry was made for the elite White society. They were made for the people who would carry respect for this fine jewelry. They would wear it and wear it with pride without looking at the bulkiness of it. They looked at the skills that went into the crafting of it. The Navajo people, whenever they began to work with silver, used heavy gauge and they had the ability to work with heavy gauge. Not that I am saying that the Zunis can't but that was their trade—big bulky chunks of turquoise. But the traders saw the patience of the Zunis.

There are a couple of stores in Gallup that used to carry a lot of fine Zuni jewelry and I always used to wonder where it all went. This was marketed back in the East to the very elite and their friends, and maybe it filtered on down to their friends. I used to wonder where in the heck did all that jewelry go that my parents were making. I guess that's what led me to read up on some of this, and I talked to Vanderwagen and some of the old traders who used to be here when I was still going to school. I wondered where the money came from, I wondered whether it was ever going to stop. Because if it did, where were we going to get this and that? It used to scare me—how am I going to make a living if all of a sudden this is to stop? For that reason, I guess, I looked and did a little bit of research here and there and that's how I view Zuni jewelry as coming about and being one of the finest fine arts.

One of the detrimental things that came about in the late 1960s was when some tribes said that they lost their identity, they lost their heritage, and there was a move on to reintroduce the Indian arts and crafts—and this is when silversmithing and everything else really perked up. I think it really put a demand on our market. Now I think our people are struggling with the business.

JIM: Do you like the way that Zuni jewelry is changing? You have needlepoint that is so extraordinarily fine and so consistent that it looks machine-made even though it's handmade, and there is jewelry so fine that sometimes people call it micro-inlay and it is so careful that, like you were saying, you look at it from across the room and can't tell what the design is. In the case of the older designs, like your parents', you look at it from across the room and you can easily see that it is a Knifewing or it is a Rainbow. How do you understand those kinds of changes in Zuni jewelry? And do you appreciate them?

CHARLES: Well, I appreciate the fact that people are taking pride in their work. But, if I do my job and take pride in it, I will keep on improving. And that is how I believe each Zuni craftsman feels about their work. We have other people who copy our work. And people come and tell me that a certain piece is mine, and it doesn't have my stamp on it. The argument they give is that they bought it a long time ago before I started using a stamp on it. But I recognize my work and can say that it is not mine and will be truthful about it. And sometimes I would take other people's work and repair it, but it got to be cumbersome and once they hear about it they will always bring the same style of work that my wife and I are doing and want it repaired.

I charge a little for my work now, I always have. I didn't really go sky-high when the jewelry was booming so I didn't suffer. I stay within my means and I realized that sooner or later this thing was going to bottom out. If I maintain my quality of work and maintain my skills, then I can always carry on the livelihood of making jewelry.

I guarantee my work and whenever something goes wrong—like if a stone comes out—I will repair it free. But if they dismantled the whole thing, and I can't really fix it, then I will make another one and charge them the same amount.

I have gone to a little bit of heavier gauge to avoid these problems. Now I am looking at the general market and I have gotten away from the concept of the elite market—to the competitive world.

JIM: In this century, we have come to see Hopi work as overlay, we have come to see Navajo work as stamped silver and cast silver, and we have come to see Zuni work as primarily lapidary—the grinding, fitting, and polishing of stones. Why do you think that is true? Why don't we see more stamped work here in Zuni? Why don't we see heavier silver? Why don't we see overlay? Why is there the emphasis in Zuni on fitting colored stones?

CHARLES: I believe the Zuni people want to maintain their identity through the crafts that they started off with. Now, this is where I am going to kind of get critical about Navajo people. Navajo people are out there to make money. Their basic history in silver making is working with heavy gauge silver, stamped work, and sandcasting. For us, I think it has to do with tribal pride that we don't want to copy anybody's work. Although we would slightly differentiate our family's work from others, Zunis basically do the same kind of work here.

JIM: You started to say that you didn't want to be critical of the Navajos, but . . .

CHARLES: They will try anything. I think this has something to do with the sweatshops and the backroom type of manufacturing that some traders do. They want to mass produce and make a fast buck. I don't think it is the Navajo people at their will but, well, they pick it up and they say to themselves, "I learned how to do it here, and I will go on my own and start doing it." I think that is how this thing developed and you see a lot of Zuni-style work that is being done by Navajo people. They are into Hopi overlay. They are into making Hopi and Zuni kachina dolls. They are into making fetishes.

This is the way a Navajo elder told me one time when I was working for the Forest Service. He asked me for a fetish, and my dad used to make fetishes sometimes. He would look at a stone and if he sees there was something he could make out of it then he would do it. That's how I do it sometimes. I don't take a block and cut it then shape it. My parents had taught me to be conservative in that area so I will look at a stone and shape it and not grinding anyway the excess, but shape it. And the Navajo when he asked me about a fetish I said, "Yeah my father makes them sometimes" and said, "Why?" He said, "I want one of a horse and one of a cow and a sheep." In those days it was a valued thing that they used, I guess, in their religious

ceremonies for prosperity in livestock—that's what he told me. As far as I knew from that day the Navajos didn't make fetishes and now you have Navajos making fetishes claiming that they have made fetishes all their life, that their grandparents made fetishes.

JIM: So, you are saying that Zunis are staying within stone work because that is identified as Zuni work and to do something else would be to do Hopi or Navajo or even Anglo work? But, why do you suppose that Zuni jewelry has come to be identified as lapidary—this colorful use of stones that are carefully fit into a pattern?

CHARLES: I think that it is in part because of a demand out there, and I think that people have begun to realize what is Zuni work.

I am a silversmith and I have an ability to do just about anything that I want to. And if I make a piece of nugget jewelry—and I don't make nugget jewelry—and I want to sell it, you would question where I got it, because that is not me, that is not my work, though I have the ability to do it. Also, we have a family tradition, a line of work, and we maintain our identity through our craft livelihood.

Going back to the earlier question that you asked about some big jewelry that I wear. As I said, this is a sign of prestige and there are some Zunis who can find big pieces of turquoise that they make into jewelry for ceremonial wear—it is not a daily wear. That's something that you look at it and it's nice when you are doing the social dances and our ceremonial dances when the kachinas are dressed with big silver pins. My dad also used to make these squash blossoms, and he created his own stamps.

He would do this and that to keep the bread and butter on the table. Like, if I don't have demand for my jewelry that I am making right now—and didn't have the skills to go hunt for a job—then I would probably do something different. That's how my dad was. For a while he was making squash blossoms, then when the market demand

Figure 204. Alonzo Hustito with house jewelry in his workshop

increased for the other kind of work, then they would go and do that kind of work.

JIM: One of the ways to understand jewelry is how it is used. So you mentioned that there are large pieces with large pieces of turquoise that are used for dressing the kachinas, but I have a sense that Zunis don't seem dressed unless they are wearing jewelry. The men need to wear bolo ties and when they go to Gallup maybe concho belts. And women need to wear bracelets and earrings and rings and necklaces. Why do you think that this is characteristic of Zunis? Why do they want to wear jewelry?

CHARLES: It is fashionable. White people like to wear their tie with their diamond pin, and now a gold chain is fashionable. It's the same way with us. I remember that my mother used to put on her squash blossom when she would go in to Gallup

and now she would just put on a small choker or something like that, or put on her favorite bracelets, just like ladies in any society. It's a matter of taste. At one time I started wearing a choker and everybody started wearing a choker so I took it off! With some people, and for some families, that is just the way they are. My dad used to wear a bolo all the time (Fig. 204).

JIM: Do you think it's also saying, "I am Zuni and I'm wearing Zuni jewelry?"

CHARLES: I don't know, I have worn this bolo so long, people identify me with this. At one point, I wore my Knifewing and they kind of take a second look me. They said, "Who did you sell your bolo to?" Everybody is trying to buy it, just to kid me around.

JIM: In a way its not only Zuni jewelry, it's your jewelry, it's Charles Hustito's jewelry. You come to identify jewelry as part of who they are, because that's what they wear.

CHARLES: I don't think anybody has another piece like this [the bolo he is wearing]. It's one of a kind. Sometimes when I make a bolo, buckle, or something like that, it's a one of a kind and I never produce it again. If you see another one like it, it's somebody else that copied it.

JIM: How long have you been wearing that bolo?

CHARLES: Let's see, my dad gave it to me when I came back out of the service in 1967, and I've been wearing it ever since then.

JIM: So it's a piece made by your father. What kind of turquoise?

CHARLES: I don't know. I never did ask him. As far as I can remember, this piece of turquoise always used to be in his toolbox—he used to have this toolbox where he had all his silversmith tools in it. There was another big piece of coral that he later on made into a bowguard. I have that bowguard too. I have that piece of coral (Fig.200).

The turquoise in the bolo used to be one piece. At one time some man borrowed it and used it for a ceremonial. They didn't tie it too well and it broke loose and dropped and shattered. But he put it back together and then he made a bolo out of it. I remember this stone used to be in the toolbox for a long time. It's always been in this leaf shape—he shaped it I don't know when. One time I told him, "Dad, don't ever sell it or don't give it away." I said, "Someday when I make enough money I want to buy it from you." When I got out of the service he gave it to me. I could never sell it. Sometimes I'm kind of scared because I don't polish it anymore with the machines. When it gets tarnished I take some soap and toothbrush and polish it back up. But if I keep polishing it with the polishing wheel, it's going to wear out, and I don't want that. The bowguard, the big coral he had a bowguard made out of it way back in the fifties by a man named

Dan Simplicio. He used to do nugget type of work. He made it for him.

JIM: Could I take it to a photo studio—so I might be gone for two or three days. Would that be possible?

CHARLES: I don't know! Huh, huh [keeps on laughing] I don't know, I'm afraid I'll be lost without it. It's just kind of got to be a habit. Sometimes I forget to take it off. Like last night I came home—it was kind of late, cold wind was blowing—I went out and started chopping wood. When I came in my wife got after me. I said; "Well it's just a part of me, sometimes I forget to take it off."

Well I hope I filled in the gaps about Zuni jewelry. I've always said that one of these days I'm going to do a book and I still might—from a different perspective, from a Zuni's point of view. I used to talk to the traders a lot sometimes—well, especially to this one gentleman, Ed Vanderwagen and wife, Dena Vanderwagen. They've both passed away. Ed was like, I guess like a father, like a grandfather and like a, well, a good friend. He treated me real nice and his wife treated me real nice. So I've always had admiration, respect, for them. Even after Ed passed away, I used to see his wife quite a bit sometimes—she was around the village or in Gallup, and I'll stop by and talk with her. They're wonderful people. You'll find plenty of those kind of people. Most of those Vanderwagens were born here, so they were part of Zuni. Ed spoke Zuni very fluently and he always told me, "Whatever you do, wherever you go, don't ever forget your language." Back in those days, Zuni was our primary language. And I learned Zuni fluently, and I went to school, went off the reservation at a young age.

PART V A CONVERSATION BETWEEN

MILFORD NAHOHAI AND

JIM OSTLER

MILFORD NAHOHAI AND JIM OSTLER (FIG. 205) MANAGE THE PUEBLO OF ZUNI ARTS AND CRAFTS ENTERPRISE. IN WHAT FOLLOWS, JIM IS PRIMARILY ASKING THE QUESTIONS AND MILFORD IS PRIMARILY PROVIDING THE ANSWERS. THE QUESTIONS TRY TO GET AT WHAT CONSTITUTES ZUNI DESIGN IN JEWELRY AND HOW IT CONTRASTS WITH OTHER JEWELRY USING THE SAME MATERIALS. THE QUESTIONS ARE ALSO DIRECTED AT CHANGES IN ZUNI JEWELRY AND THE NATURE OF OUTSIDE INFLUENCE.

ALTHOUGH SOME OF MILFORD'S VIEWS MAY NOT BE SHARED BY ALL ZUNIS, THEY ARE GIVEN BY A ZUNI WHO HAS BECOME VERY KNOWLEDGEABLE ABOUT ZUNI JEWELRY AND WHO, IN HIS DAILY WORK, MUST ASSESS THE MARKET VALUE OF A CONSIDERABLE AMOUNT OF JEWELRY THAT PASSES BEFORE HIM. THE PURPOSE OF THE INTERVIEW WAS TO TALK ABOUT ZUNI VALUES WHICH ARE PRESUMED BY, AND ARTICULATED WITHIN, ZUNI JEWELRY.

Figure 205. Milford Nahohai and Jim Ostler

JIM: We were both struck by the clarity of something your mom said. "Make yourself of value, by wearing something of value." What were the circumstances when she said that—what were you doing and what did she see? What did she mean?

MILFORD: I think it was the jewelry that I was wearing, and it wasn't Zuni jewelry. It was the gold that I was wearing. On one arm I had about five bracelets on and she made a point, saying that I was just like this certain man who used to adorn himself a lot. I can't remember that man's name. I told her, "Well, they are valuable." She used that term, *Do' kwa hoł deh'uliu do' dehyak'yanna*, meaning when you wear something of value you will be valued. I guess by the ancestors. It is hard to translate it back, but I think that's what the whole thing was about. She said that she got the phrase from her aunt who told her about it and told her that she should always wear something that is valuable. It doesn't necessarily have to be gold or diamonds.

I guess after she was told that statement she always wore a necklace or a bracelet or something, not just for going out or going to dances or dressing up to go to town, but just in her daily life. I don't think she even took her necklaces off in the nightime. I have always seen her going to bed and that is what she wore.

Figure 206. Josephine Nahohai

JIM: Can you describe those necklaces?

MILFORD: They were Navajo necklaces—all silver graduated beads. The center had a real large ball and the others graduated in size. It was just a little choker. It didn't really hang down, just around her neck. She used to wear that one until she gave it away to a friend. The next thing she started wearing was a fetish necklace. They were little bears carved out of bone and they were strung on coral. That is what she always wore until this past summer when she gave it away to a friend. I don't know if she is wearing any necklaces. Well, she's got a little turquoise choker, so she is wearing that right now. But besides that on her neck she always has her pins on, her bracelets, and her earrings on (Fig. 206).

JIM: Are these Zuni pieces?

MILFORD: All the jewelry that she is wearing right now are Zuni pieces. The one that I gave her was the Sunface pendant by Benji and Shirley Tzuni (Fig. 207). And then a bracelet that her clan sister gave to her, Eleanor. It's like an old-style bracelet. I think it's a single row. And then she has got on her rings. She's got some rings on that are 14 carat that our oldest brother's wife and he had done. And the other ring that she wears is also 14 carat.

I got her the earrings so many years ago in Gallup, and I don't know if they are even Indian made. But they had Persian turquoise. She lost one side—the dangle part on it. I gave the remaining earrings to Harlan and Rolanda Coonsis and they made a ring out of it for her. That's what she is always wearing now—that ring (Fig. 208).

JIM: Why do you suppose that she said, "Make yourself of value, by wearing something of value" when you were wearing a number of gold bracelets? Why do think she said it when she did?

MILFORD: I think that she was trying to say that I should wear something all the time and not just when dressing up for an occasion. A lot of people

Figure 207. Sunface pin by Benji and Shirley Tzuni

Figure 208. Gold ring adapted from earring by Rolanda Haloo

Figure 209. Navajo inlay ring

dress up for occasions, but I guess she wanted to say it's all right to be wearing stuff like this all the time, to integrate it into your daily life. That's the way I would understand it. But the best way I would find out would be to ask her directly.

JIM: Did you take it as criticism?

MILFORD: I don't think it was criticism. Or, maybe . . . no, I don' t think it was put in that way because after she told me that then my other nephew started looking around to see what he could wear, too.

JIM: You have always, more or less in a joking manner—but there is a serious side to it—been critical of a prominent Navajo designer's jewelry. This jewelry is inlay: colored stones, finely cut, and set in certain kinds of patterns. What do you see that makes this jewelry—that looks so Zuni to a casual observer—different? Why are you critical of this jewelry?

MILFORD: I guess to an outsider the looks of his jewelry is just seen as inlay. Where I am more critical is how the designing has been done. To

me when I see the inlay done by Zunis there is sort of like a set pattern, or they try to make some kind of a design—I don't know if that's the word—some kind of pattern that I think they have seen around Zuni. I just see him putting in stones, colorful stones. I like the use of color he has, but somehow to me it just doesn't look Zuni. That's not to say that it is Zuni work that he is trying to do.

JIM: You suggest that it doesn't have a pattern that you can see—it just becomes inlay and colored stones, maybe more random and without any pattern.

MILFORD: It doesn't have the pattern or, what do you call it, the feel that some of the Zuni craftsmen really put into their work. And besides, when we talk about this designed jewelry, is it work that he actually did or is it his craftsmen that are doing the work for him? There are some pieces, like some of the earlier pieces that I have seen, that he says he designed—but he had some Zuni boys working under him that were doing those pieces. And some of the pieces I liked. I do own one of

Figure 210. Manufactured bracelet

Figure 211. Bolo by Oliver Cellicion

his bracelets. But I just got it to show the difference in the style of the work and how the whole process is (Fig. 210).

JIM: What is there that you see about Zuni work that makes you feel that it includes the feeling of the craftsmen?

MILFORD: In the Zuni work I guess I would probably say when I hold the pieces and look over the design itself if it is, sort of, like uniform.

JIM: Who brings in work to sell at the Enterprise that has real good feel so that you could use their work as an example?

MILFORD: Well, probably some of the people who do the Sunfaces—like the Niiha family, Esther Lonjose Niiha. I would say that about her pieces, because sometimes she has brought pieces where the stones have not been set right and I will ask her what the deal is this time? And she will talk about how she was in a rush and wasn't herself when she was working on these pieces and I will tell her to bring some other pieces when she is in a better mood.

JIM: And with the Navajo designer's work I presume that you are not talking about craftsmanship, because his pieces seem to fit well. What you are talking about is the way he puts the pieces together?

MILFORD: I think that his work is sort of just random. To me, there is not really a set pattern. To me it is just like he wants to use up the space and put in the stones.

Two years ago they had that Zuni show in Flagstaff [at the Museum of Northern Arizona] and I got there on the last day. The people that ran the museum got hold of me. They started taking me around to the different award winners and were asking my comments. When I got to the piece that was done by a prominent Zuni artist, I had to ask who the judges were to give that piece an award. My comment was that it was a Zuni trying to do Navajo inlay—meaning the stones were randomly put in, they didn't really go with the color. Certain colors will blend in with each other, but this was just a piece where it was all pieced together just by different colored stones. And that was my comment—it was a Zuni trying to do Navajo inlay. Again, they asked me to try to explain and I just told them, "It just didn't look right."

JIM: So, you see a clear distinction between Navajo inlay and Zuni inlay and you feel it immediately?

MILFORD: Yep. Like, when I go to different shops where it is marked as Zuni I can tell if it is not Zuni. And right now there are some Zunis who are going to Gallup and buying preset stones and they do have a Navajo feel [laughter] because it is Navajos who are doing the stone cutting and the Zunis are just setting them. It is prefabricated.

JIM: These are pieces where the stone has been cut and they have already been set into a kind of pattern or no pattern?

MILFORD: Yes. All they do is just get it and mount it on top of a ring shank and that's it. So, that's, the reason, I guess, I still like the old-style mosaic inlay 'cause there's not that many people still doing that. A lot of them are doing the multi-color inlay here in Zuni and to me it is getting to be more like what you see in Gallup—the prefabricated stuff. They are doing more on that route. But there are some others still doing the old-style mosaic inlay where you can see the certain patterns they are trying to work with.

JIM: Certain patterns and color and the lightness and darkness of the stone and the way that it comes together and makes a coherent piece?

MILFORD: They all fit together, all go into one.

JIM: And that's what you call old-style mosaic inlay, as opposed to new style or Navajo?

MILFORD: Yes. When I see that new style or Navajo it is more like a rush job. 'Cause what they are doing is just fitting the stones together (Fig. 209).

Figure 212. *Sha'lak'o* bolo by Rosalie Pinto

In the old-style mosaic inlay you have cloud patterns or lightning patterns or triangle patterns that can be like that—but they will make an overall different pattern on the piece (Fig. 35). What is out there now, the new inlay, the Navajo style, they are just put in, they don't really have a pattern yet. Some of the earlier Gasper pieces were different. It seemed like they took a little more time in making their pieces, but now—I guess because of the demand for their work—they are just sort of mass-producing their work sort of like a sweatshop. I usually make comments to both of the Gasper brothers that I would like to see some of the earlier work again where each piece was really more unique instead of all fitting the same pattern. Right now, I am seeing from those two the same pattern as far as the stones have been put in—the only difference is the coloration of the stones.

JIM: Could you talk some more about composition?

MILFORD: It is sort of like I tell my nephew who is learning to paint pottery. The first stuff that I saw from him I said, "Yeah it is good, but you need to work on your lines, using thick lines, medium lines, thin lines, so that way everything all fits in right together." I told him that the key was the execution of design, the use of lines. There are different types of lines that he can use. I think that he understood what I was saying because in his later pieces I started to see what I wanted to see.

JIM: And with respect to some of the newer Zuni work, [a particular Zuni artist who makes a banded inlay bracelet was mentioned] do you see it falling in this kind of rushed inlay or . . . ?

MILFORD: Yeah, he is still under the influence of the Navajo designer where he just puts the stones in and there's hardly any designing—it's just colored stones put in.

JIM: Can you think of a good example of mosaic inlay?

MILFORD: I would say pieces by Oliver Cellecion (Fig. 211), Thomasine Shack, Mary Kalestewa, some of Ed Beyuka's earlier pieces, Rosalie Pinto's earlier pieces (Fig. 212), and the late Alonzo Hustito's work. What they did first was the stone cutting and put the pattern on a cardboard. Then, after the stone work was finished they would do the silver work.

And I think I still have one set like that. It was my dad's. I forget who made it. It was a Rainbow Man that was done for him. The stone work was already done and it was put on cardboard and all you needed to do was put it on silver.

JIM: As opposed to what is happening now?

MILFORD: I haven't really seen any of the people who are doing the inlay, as far as how they are doing their stone work. Some of the pieces are not actually soldered in. They'll just put a strip of silver in at the same time they are doing the stone work. I think that is the difference that I see now.

Figure 213. House jewelry

People like Andrew Dewa are still doing that mosaic inlay and you can see that it takes longer for them to do it (Figs. 156–158).

JIM: Andrew Dewa's work has a three-dimensional relief.

MILFORD: Most of the older pieces are like that, too. They are more three-dimensional, judging on what I have seen from the museum collections.

JIM: What about someone like Alonzo Hustito? How do you see Erma Hustito's work relating?

MILFORD: What I have seen from Erma are the bracelets. They didn't really have the same technique as her father's work—meaning that it was more of the contemporary, there wasn't really overall design on it. It was almost like looking at Charles Loloma's work—the skyscraper style. That to me was sort of the pattern that she had on her pieces.

JIM: How do you regard Charles Loloma's work?

MILFORD: When I first saw some of his pieces I liked them, 'cause they were simple but still had a Hopi feel. There were some rings that I saw that he had cast and he just accented them with maybe one stone or maybe a diamond. But that one stone, and the way it was positioned, really accented the pieces. The thing that I didn't like about his work were those bracelets—the skyscraper bracelets—they were jagged.

The stones were not coming out even. They were nice looking, but I didn't think that anyone from Zuni would wear anything like that because some of the pieces were too chunky looking or too massive. If a Zuni would have worn it for something over here—for maybe dancing or stuff like that—it would have gotten in the way, or the stones would have gotten hit somehow and they would break. You see some of the dancers all decked out in jewelry and the way they are rough on the jewelry—the pieces are still done good and they don't really break that much.

JIM: It still is interesting to me what your mother said about jewelry that you wear all the time becoming part of you. But, is there not jewelry that Zunis make and value, for example, large squash blossom necklaces, that is not worn every day? I have even heard someone refer to that as the house jewelry and that it belonged to the house—for successive generations of women who live in that house to wear (Fig. 213). Is there everyday jewelry and also jewelry that you wouldn't wear everyday—that you would use to dress up?

MILFORD: I think there is everyday jewelry—like what I see my mom wearing, her rings and her earrings and her brooches.

Some of the stuff that you don't see everyday—I think that the only time that is worn is during special occasions here in Zuni, otherwise if they are going to a graduation or going into town—especially if it is like a big event like Gallup Ceremonial or State Fair where the older folks want to dress themselves out. That's when you start seeing the squashes coming out—and some of the older men might even put on their concho belts or thick clusters of necklaces.

JIM: What are the differences between these kinds of jewelry?

MILFORD: I think that the jewelry that the people would use to dress up would be the older pieces or the heavier pieces. They are displaying the jewelry, they are not actually going to be working in it. Everyday jewelry is more like smaller pieces or lightweight jewelry. The person wearing it does not know that they are wearing it—it is just part of them. You can tell when they have real big squash on or a big bracelet on—eventually they will start talking about how heavy it is getting.

JIM: Do you think that your mom could have been alluding to the fact that you only had everyday jewelry, and you needed to get some better pieces?

MILFORD: It could be. I have been getting jewelry that would be classified as being for special events—meaning that I have been buying the chunkier stuff, and heavier bracelets, bigger bolos. But there are a couple of pieces that I would be wearing everyday if I wanted to 'cause they are light. The thing is, they are different, and if I wear them I will be getting a lot of attention from not only non-Zunis but Zunis themselves. They are always wondering what stone it is and everything like that.

JIM: I saw some new pieces by Harlan Coonsis, including a parrot. I liked the colorful inlay on the wing—and Rolanda Haloo's pieces as they evolved. How would you characterize their jewelry in terms of this old and new inlay?

MILFORD: I still see some of those pieces—like the dragonflies by Rolanda Haloo—as mosaic inlay. Whereas Harlan—when he is using the Knifewing—is doing the newer inlay. Some of the older pieces would be three-dimensional, but Harlan's are all flat.

That is also true of Rolanda's, but I think the work on the wings itself is still the old-style mosaic inlay. To me, old-style mosaic inlay is like a puzzle where you are working on the puzzle first and then doing the silver work last, even though

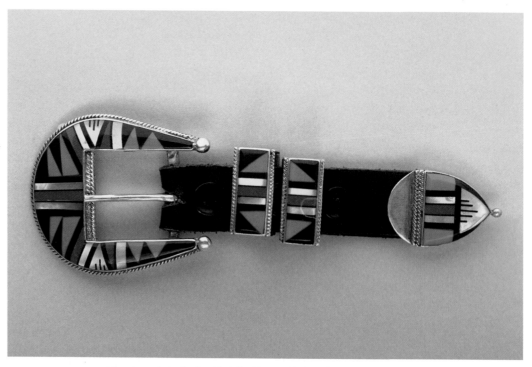

Figure 214. Imitation Zuni belt buckle set. Made in the Philippines with plastic turquoise and coral

Rolanda does do the silver work first and sets the stones in last.

JIM: Your job has enabled you to travel all around the world and to go to large trade shows where you see jewelry from virtually every place in the world. You also see jewelry which is imitation Zuni. Can you easily spot work that is imitation Zuni? What it is that allows you to conclude that this is not Zuni.

MILFORD: I think that with overseas items—from the Philippines or Thailand—I can distinguish just by glancing that it is imitation. The metal has a different effect and the stones are just too blue to be turquoise. In the imitation they don't really use turquoise—they mostly use plastic (Fig. 214). The finish just doesn't look right.

JIM: The finish? In terms of . . . ?

MILFORD: The stones, the metal itself—the metal sometimes looks too dull and doesn't even look like silver, but like some base metal.

JIM: Some of the pieces are actually copies of particular Zuni pieces? And even here you can tell?

MILFORD: On some pieces I can tell right away. On some pieces I have to look closer at it—the thing that tells me to take an extra look is usually the stone work.

JIM: More than ten years ago, when we were doing photography for our brochures, we went to see Thelma Sheche and her granddaughters. We had brought over a fairly large amount of jewelry. We asked Thelma and her granddaughters if they would put on some jewelry so we could take some photographs. They were dressed in traditional mantas. What really struck me on that occasion was that when we asked these girls to select some pieces—maybe one was nine and the other twelve—was the amount of jewelry they put on. They didn't just put on one necklace, they put on three or four necklaces, several pin pendants, and several rings (Fig. 98). So that made me think that Zuni jewelry must mean something more than design and be more than an accessory.

MILFORD: Well, to me it was good that Thelma wore all that jewelry but, as for the daughters, to me they sort of overdid it because the outfits they wore were not ones that could really show off the jewelry.

I think that outfits have a say in what jewelry is worn. Some of the pieces that they put on—you couldn't actually see them. If they were dressed in the manta outfit then I think it would have been better looking.

JIM: They didn't have mantas on?

MILFORD: No, they had *mihe:we* on.

JIM: So there was too much background interference? A manta would have been all black and would have made things stand out?

MILFORD: The jewelry couldn't really be seen, yeah.

JIM: What of the fact that the girls put on so much jewelry?

MILFORD: Well, it's just that they are still young girls and they got a chance to dress up.

JIM: I see Anglo ladies who buy Zuni earrings that will match their blouse. But, when I see Zunis wearing jewelry, it seems far more significant.

MILFORD: I think it's a display of their wealth. I think the term *wasudena:we* meaning "material wealth." The tribal seal has a picture of a squash blossom necklace and the words *u ten nawa*. I think that it is the way older folks see jewelry— *udena:we*, as part of their wealth.

JIM: Do you think that accounts for the size of some of the jewelry, for example, the larger squashes (Fig. 204)?

MILFORD: I think so, because most of those are older pieces and there was an abundance of turquoise.

JIM: When an Alice Quam piece came into the Enterprise—a beautiful large and well-matched squash—one particular female staff member, Mary Ghahate, couldn't stand not to have it (Fig. 215). Regardless of what Mary had in her trunk of jewelry—she had to have it. Even if it meant laying it

away, she had to have it. Can you try to explain that? What's that person doing?

MILFORD: I think it's the older pieces—the squashes, the manta pins—that are really needed in the household, for dancing and stuff like that. That's why it is borrowed a lot. I know that within our family, when there is dancing going on, they usually borrow my mom's larger squashes, larger bracelets, and larger manta pins. And I think that would be true with most families here.

In the case of Rolanda Haloo's pieces—the workmanship is detailed and you really have to get up close to look at it and to understand the whole design. With the older pieces, the clusterwork, you can be off at a distance and it still catches. The cluster pieces and the older pieces can go well with both the traditional outfits and the modern outfits too. I don't think Rolanda's dragonflies would stand out on a traditional piece. They might stand out on contemporary clothing but not on a traditional piece, because when you wear the more traditional stuff it would sort of get lost. When you see older Navajos, that's what they are wearing—the cluster pieces. I gave an Alice Quam piece to my friend for graduation and all those Navajos ladies up there they started—I don't know what they were saying because they were all talking in their own language—but they all appreciated that piece and they started joking around, saying that one of them was retiring at a certain time, and was she going to expect something like that if I come to her dinner [laughter].

JIM: This was a Navajo friend at Crownpoint, N.M.?

MILFORD: Yes, she graduated and I gave her an Alice Quam squash. She had on strands of turquoise, but when she opened up her squash she just immediately took them off and said that this one goes with the whole outfit. And she had on her *biil* [traditional Navajo dress].

JIM: The other piece that Mary had to buy was a Faye Quandelacy fetish necklace. What is the appeal to Zunis of her necklaces?

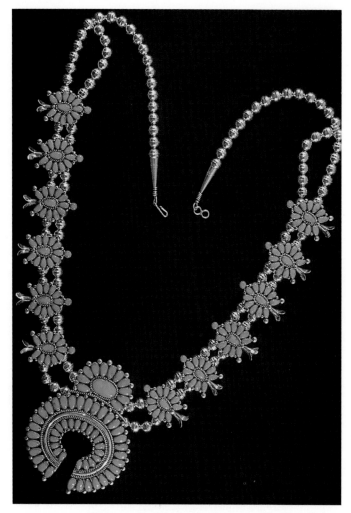

Figure 215. Necklace by Alice Quam owned by Mary Ghahate

MILFORD: It was not just because of Faye's popularity. As I recall, the necklace was eagles and Mary, being from the Eagle Clan, I think she had an attachment for that reason. That's what I usually do, too. Within our family, if we see jewelry that relates to our clans, then that's what we will get and wear. Also I know that they were carved out of fossilized ivory and the ivory had real good coloration on it. So I think that the coloration, plus the design itself, had meaning to her—symbolizing her clan membership.

JIM: You have been buying jewelry as a buyer for a large store for at least eleven years. What kinds of changes do you see taking place?

MILFORD: The Sunface used to be standard turquoise, coral, mother-of-pearl. The change that I am seeing now is the use of different stones. Maybe the design of certain pieces—I keep going back to the Sunface—when we first started, it was the basic

sun design. Now they are getting more elaborate with the designs; the feathers are getting to be more raised or they might put line work in it to make them look like the feathers of the bonnet itself.

JIM: What are some of the new stones?

MILFORD: The sugilite, the opal, the lapis, Chinese turquoise. Myself, I like—I have never really liked the bright blue turquoise—I have always liked the old turquoise, more the greener side. Earlier I was collecting a lot of the greener turquoise. But, I don't really see much of that now. That's why I am partial to Chinese turquoise right now.

JIM: Because it is greener?

MILFORD: It has an older look to it. I got a necklace for my mom and it was all done in plastic, which was set in silver—the beads were all handmade in silver and everything like that. This was a Navajo piece and the stone work was all done in plastic. But we were offered a good price for it. I told my mom that we would go ahead and get it and give it to one of our friends, and they in turn can take the plastic off and set it with Chinese turquoise. And when she did that the whole necklace has a whole different look to it. It looks like a real older piece, and when she wears it a lot of people think that it is an antique piece.

JIM: One of the things that boggles my mind about, for example, an Alice Quam piece (Fig. 215) or an Edith Tsabetsaye piece (Fig. 129) is that the stones are so perfect and so evenly matched. Yet the stones come from a material that is so variable—every section is different in color, value, and hue from all others. A Zuni artist has not only shaped these stones so that they are all the same, but they have made it so that the color is consistent throughout a large necklace. Why do Zunis do that?

MILFORD: I think everything has to be matched. It just has to be perfect to their eyes. It just has to go—they all have to fit together. They all have to, sort of, become one. And they all have to be even.

It's just like when the ladies themselves dress in their traditional clothing—their shoes have to be just perfectly wrapped up. If they think they are finished with a boot and they look at it and there is a crease, they have to undo it and do it all over again. With the manta, the pattern has to be a certain length from the manta itself. It has to be all even (Figs. 99 and 216). When you go to the other pueblos, you see they just sort of throw it on themselves. Their mantas are sort of sagging, their boots are sagging—and that's when Zunis talk about how poorly dressed they are.

A couple of years ago we had some friends at Acoma who were taking part in the Corn Dance. The daughters requested to have my Mom and her sister over there to dress them up, to make them stand out in the crowd—they said that they wanted to dress like a Zuni.

So, of course, my mom and her sister went out and looked at their clothing. The way they had their manta pins lined up on their mantas wasn't correct so they redid their mantas. Well, they dressed them up like they dress themselves—the Zuni style—and the girls were talking about a lot of comments they got from all the other ladies; saying that they were properly dressed, that they were dressed real neat. The ladies asked who dressed them and they said, "Our aunts from Zuni." And the ladies said, "Oh, we should have known." It's just like, you know, everything has to come out perfectly.

JIM: I was wondering about the influence of women in Zuni silversmithing? Do you see any difference in work done by women and work done by men?

MILFORD: Not really, 'cause it's hard to tell who does what unless it is just an individual working by himself—then I would be able to make a distinction—but most of the jewelry that we see is a combination of both the husband and the wife.

JIM: Do you see any occupational specialization by gender?

Figure 216. Caroline Othole

Figure 217. Inlay pendant by Yelmo Natachu

MILFORD: Right now, the women are the ones who are doing more of the stone setting—the lapidary—and the husbands do the silver work.

JIM: Do you think that each of them has skills in the other area as well?

MILFORD: I think so. Take, for instance, Rolanda and Harlan Coonsis. With Rolanda's family it was always the females who did the stone setting and I guess her father was the one who did the metal work. That sort of passed on with Harlan and Rolanda.

I was talking with Harlan a few years ago and he was frustrated. He wanted to work on stones but Rolanda wouldn't really give him an opportunity. Eventually, Harlan started doing some of his own pieces where he was doing stone settings. Rolanda still had an influence on him about how to have the stones set in, what degree they had to be cut, and everything like that—to make sure it fit her standards.

That's the only example that I know of. I think it is basically that way with all her sisters. I think all of her sisters all do the stone work and their husbands are the ones who do the silver work.

JIM: Zuni jewelry is sold everywhere and 99 percent of the buyers are White people. If Zuni jewelry is being made for an outside audience, does it cease to be Zuni jewelry?

MILFORD: I don't think so.

JIM: How would you answer the critic who says that the market is primarily controlled by White people and that they determine what designs are made.

MILFORD: I don't really see them having the control on the design. I think the Zuni people still have the control over the designs. Maybe suggestions are given for different kinds of stones, but the basic design is still controlled by the Zunis themselves.

I think that one time a company designed a line of jewelry that was supposed to be made for them—

that was an exclusive line for a certain company. Other than that, I think the majority of the craftsmen here do their own designs.

I know that we don't dictate to our craftsmen here. We let them do what they want to do. Maybe we will suggest they use different stones, but as far as the whole construction of the design is concerned, I think that is still done by the craftsmen.

JIM: What was the example of a company wanting Zunis to make their design?

MILFORD: It was the Olympics [1984], and the company wanted to have all the jewelry done with the Olympic symbol on the pieces. It was a design that was brought in and given to the craftsmen, and the craftsmen had to follow the measurements on what the design looked like.

JIM: How did that work out?

MILFORD: I don't think it was that good. I talked with some people and they said that it didn't really take off that much. They were expecting huge orders to come in but they never materialized.

JIM: Recently, Loretta Weahkee [who works on the wholesale marketing side for Arts and Crafts] has been working on developing a market for Christian jewelry—particularly crosses set into mosaic inlay pattern (Fig. 217). Is that Zuni work? Is it Christian work? Is it outside work?

MILFORD: I would say that technically it is still Zuni work, the only thing is they had to make an adaptation of making the cross bolder. The only thing, you know, that made it Christian looking was just the cross that was done inside. The lapidary that was around it was still Zuni work.

JIM: Do you see Zuni jewelry changing to meet the tastes of Anglo or non-Native American buyers?

MILFORD: A couple of years back, maybe a year or two ago, we started seeing all of these multicolor stones coming in. I know that the manufacturers were producing the multicolor stones and some of the buyers started suggesting to the craftsmen here that they use them. And I started seeing them bringing in pieces which we had bought earlier that were single color but now they were all multicolor stones. I think a few people will do something like that just as a fad, but basically Zunis dictate their own designs.

JIM: In the case of multicolors, when you look at them do they look Zuni to you?

MILFORD: Designwise it is, but to me it has sort of the manufactured look to it. It's manufactured because the use of stones was being dictated by some person other than the artists themselves.

JIM: So what are the qualities that Zuni jewelry has that it doesn't have? Manufactured to you not only means that it was made in a factory, but it also means that it is not creative, it is not sensitive, and it doesn't have pattern. So in its look, in its appearance, what does it lack so that you call it manufactured?

MILFORD: Maybe the uniformity. When Zunis do certain things, like when they do the cluster-work, they make sure that all the stones are matched up with the same coloration. When you use different stones you won't get the uniformity. I think that what I am trying to get to is . . . that it's not all there.

JIM: I have seen you go and look at the work being sold in outlets run by other dealers and you will look at a piece and say, "Ehhh, it looks manufactured." And though you have no idea who made the piece, what you are basing your assessment on is that it doesn't look like it was made by an artist who has combined color and design in the stones. So what is it about a particular dealer's jewelry that makes it look manufactured?

MILFORD: I would say the look—the look of the piece itself, and also the creativity. Some of them I don't like, especially when they put a patina on some of their finishes to make them look like they were old pieces.

Figure 218. Inlay bracelet by Val Banteah

JIM: If we are buying such a piece in the store, you will come over to me and quietly say, "What do you think?" And then say to me, "Oh, it looks manufactured." Why does it look manufactured?

MILFORD: The look . . . . [laughter] In Zuni jewelry, people pay a lot of attention to the finish—the silver being shiny. The dealer wants to pass them off as antique pieces and again it is going back to the look.

JIM: I also think that you are talking about the way that they select and set the stones, the kinds of groupings that they create.

MILFORD: Yes. I have started seeing cabs (precut stones for setting) that have multifacets on them. I haven't seen anybody doing that here before. The ones that are doing it, they just bought the cabs themselves which have been mass-produced.

JIM: Whereas, in Zuni jewelry, each piece is different from every other piece, each craftsman is different from every other craftsman?

MILFORD: Yes, and even though they might bring into the store pieces with the same pattern, still the stone work might be different. There will be changes of stones here and there, but the overall design will still look the same.

JIM: If the buyer dictates exactly how the pieces are supposed to be—the size, the dimension, the color, the transitions—then it becomes repetitive. Even though Zuni pieces repeat—we all know that the Hustitos have their style, and the Ukestines, and every family has their own style—still the work does not look manufactured.

MILFORD: On some of them you can see that there are just repetitious designs—especially the manufactured stuff. You just have one, you sell it, and you can just dig in the box and pick another one out and replace it. With Zuni jewelry you might look for similar design, but the stone work will not be the same. Even though it might be all in turquoise, they use different kinds of turquoise—one might have a lot of matrix, another not much at all. It will always be different.

JIM: And so for you when you look at Zuni jewelry you see that here an artist has put this together and has made those selections every time. So if there is matrix or not, or a change in color, it's there because the artist chose to make it this way—its form is not arbitrary. They have put it all together and have selected every little piece of stone and then they have set it. In the manufactured look it can appear arbitrary—as you were saying about some Navajo work where you felt it was just a matter of fitting stones together and other work where somebody has repeated almost stamplike the same pieces again and again. It is like buying a set of silverware where all the forks, all the spoons, and all the knives are the same. When you buy Zuni "silverwear" each piece, each single piece, is handmade. When you consider the

variability in stone it further illustrates the artist's taste and skill. Take Val Banteah's work, for example. Even though you see similar designs from piece to piece, within each piece he has orchestrated the stones so that they harmonize together (Fig. 218).

MILFORD: [silence]

JIM: Is that what you think?

MILFORD: [laughter] Yep. Thank you. [laughter]

JIM: Is there any other way to display Zuni jewelry other than wearing it? Are there Zuni equivalents to the kinds of jewelry designed and sold by Tiffany's?

MILFORD: From what I know, the jewelry made here at Zuni is only for personal adornment. It's made to be worn, and displayed, especially when we have any kind of gathering or feast day. I know that at one time it was to show our wealth. I don't know if that is true today. Well, it is true that it displays your wealth. I think that may still be it today.

JIM: Does the fact that jewelry is worn around the neck or in the ears or around the waist or on the arm have any significance?

MILFORD: Not that I know of, but it would be something to ask. You know, that's just the way that they have always been wearing Zuni jewelry. Even when a person dies they will always be loaded down with their personal jewelry—pieces that they might have selected for themselves. They have to have all that stuff with them for their afterlife.

JIM: To have jewelry?

MILFORD: Mmm umh. But, when a person dies there's a different way of putting jewelry on them, too. Like when a person dies they put a concho belt on the person but they won't use any kind of leather. If the concho belt was on a leather, they will take the leather strip off and put it on a cloth. I guess the dead person isn't allowed to be in touch with leather, so they will take all the leather off—even the moccasins. Both males and females have those black leggings on and still won't be wearing moccasins. They will take the leather off the bowguards that men wear and they will just put them on their wrist with material and fasten it on there.

JIM: We talked about jewelry in the house and how it was borrowed if somebody needed it. So, it was like someone was responsible for its care but it wouldn't so much belong to them as it belonged to the family and was loaned out to whoever needed it. Can you talk about how it is loaned out?

MILFORD: From what I know within our family it is usually borrowed by our relatives—by blood and also by clan. In our family we don't just let any person come in and say they want to borrow this for a dance or something like that. We have to look them over, to see if they are trustworthy and everything like that. If a person has a case of drinking we won't give them things like that because we assume that they will take it to a pawn shop and we won't get them back. It's just up to the individual households who they will give their items to.

Also, we will give it to another family even though we know they are not related to us. If they are responsible, we will give pieces to them and when they do borrow it, especially for a dance and stuff like that—they may have borrowed the jewelry plus all the different clothing or paraphernalia. When the dance is over, they will come to the house and give it back. Then they will offer you a little blessing, thanking you for the use of it and hope that in the long run you will be more prosperous and that you will acquire more stuff like that. So, it is an honor when you give out something and you will get something in return.

JIM: Are there times when it wouldn't be appropriate to wear jewelry?

MILFORD: Nope. I don't think so. But that's one thing I can ask my mom. But, I haven't really seen a time where they don't wear jewelry.

JIM: For example, for certain groups in periods of mourning all the jewelry may be taken off. Other groups who lead a very simple life don't want to display any personal wealth. Is there anything like that in Zuni, when on some occasion Zunis might say that this is not the time to wear jewelry?

MILFORD: I don't think so. I have never come across that.

JIM: I was trying to think about terms that could be used to describe jewelry, terms that are praiseworthy or critical.

MILFORD: *His k'okshi* would be one. *Ish aliye* means something like, "it is pretty." *Ish dikwahn okya* means it was made real good. Sometimes, when we get pieces in and it is like wasting silver, we use the term *ish k'wach'uli* meaning it is *k'wach'ulinne*, something like, "it is all lumpy."

K'wach'uli means break it or crush it, like it is lumpy, and if someone says that about your work it means that your work is not good.

BIBLIOGRAPHY

Adair, John. *The Navajo and Pueblo Silversmiths.* Norman: University of Oklahoma Press. 1944.

Chapman Papers. *Archives of the Laboratory of Anthropology.* Museum of New Mexico. Santa Fe.

Fowler, Carol. *Daisy Hooee Nampeyo, The Story of an American Indian.* Minneapolis: Dillon Press. 1977.

Hodge, Frederick W. "Turquoise Work of Hawikuh, New Mexico." *Leaflets of the Museum of the American Indian Heye Foundation New York*, 2. March 22, 1921. Reprint. Albuquerque: Calvin Horn Pub., Inc. 1974.

Jernigan, E. Wesley. *Jewelry of the Prehistoric Southwest.* School of American Research Southwest Indian Art Series. Albuquerque: University of New Mexico Press. 1978.

Judd, Neil M. "The Material Culture of Pueblo Bonito." *Smithsonian Miscellaneous Collections*, Vol. 124. Washington, D.C. 1954.

Kirk, Ruth F. "Southwestern Indian Jewelry." *El Palacio.* LII 2 (February): 21–32 and 3 (March): 41–50. 1945.

Neumann, David. "Recent Lapidary Developments at Zuni." *El Palacio.* 58 (July): 215–217. 1951.

_____ "Southwestern Indians Enter Modern Money Economy." *El Palacio.* 63 (August): 233–235. 1956.

Sikorsky, Kathryn A. *Recent Trends in Zuni Jewelry.* Master's Thesis, University of Arizona. 1958.

Sitgreaves, L. *Report of an Expedition Down the Zuni and Colorado Rivers.* Washington, D.C. 1853.

Wallace, Barbara. Unpublished manuscript on life of C.G. Wallace. n.d.

Windes, Thomas C. "Blue Notes: the Chacoan Turquoise Industry in the San Juan Basin." Ansaazi Regional Organization and the Chaco System. *Maxwell Museum of Anthropology, Anthropological Papers*, No. 8: 159–168. 1992.

INDEX